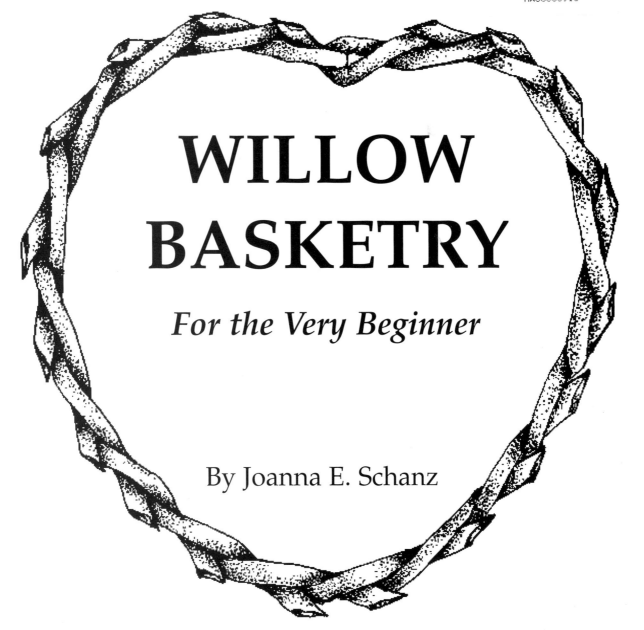

WILLOW BASKETRY

For the Very Beginner

By Joanna E. Schanz

Design by Dana Lumby

Photography by Joan Liffring-Zug Bourret

Illustrations by Joanna Schanz, Diane Heusinkveld, and Esther Feske

Editing by Dorothy Crum, Jacqueline Comito, and Jane Pesek

Penfield Press

DEDICATION

To all the students of the past who have struggled with willow. Especially the Michigan four-hour class of 1994 who struggled with me.

—Joanna E. Schanz

ISBN 1-57216-031-4
©1996 Joanna E. Schanz

TABLE OF CONTENTS

INTRODUCTION

When I began teaching in 1979, teachers and students would travel to a wild willow patch. All would cut, sort, and weave the willow to make a round willow basket during the 12- to 14-hour class.

Demand for shorter class time, and still completing a basket, required teachers to cut and sort willow for the eight-hour classes. When six-hour classes were required, all the traditional techniques of the German Amana Colony Basket could not be covered properly in the time frame. Then the four-hour class was needed. After a disastrous four-hour class (or at least what I thought would be a four-hour class), I was challenged to evaluate each willow weaving technique and to develop a class where students could experience willow and still complete a decent willow basket in a short time.

Since my husband, Norman, is a furniture craftsman for our Furniture/Refinishing Shop, I had made wooden bottom baskets before, using the native Iowa hardwoods available to me.

Woven willow bases are the hardest for students, but the first technique to learn. It was natural for the exposed, enclosed and bare bottom willow baskets to evolve. Molds do help with shaping, but are not necessary.

This book is the result of my teaching and willow experience. A book for the very beginner in willow basketmaking.

ABOUT THE AUTHOR

My willow adventure began in 1977, when Philip Dickel, the last active willow basketmaker in the Amana Colonies, helped me harvest cultured willow, sort and weave my first basket.

Since that day, I have expanded my knowledge of baskets and willows through teaching, lecturing about the Amana Colonies German Willow Basketry, and taking basketry classes from other teachers. As I grow, I find that all the knowledge I have about willow basketry and other basketry influences my weaving and will continue to do so. Using cultured willow from my willow patches, imported willow from England and Belgium, and wild willow growing in our area, I enjoy creating traditional German willow baskets and not-so traditional willow baskets.

Although I occasionally weave and teach other styles of baskets using other materials, the feel, smell, colors and natural beauty of willow give me the most pleasure.

My baskets are sold through the *Broom and Basket Shop* and the *Amana Arts Guild* in the Amana Colonies. Many are in private collections throughout the U.S. and abroad. Having traveled and studied in England, Belgium and Germany, I enjoy sharing my knowledge as I learn more.

Researching and recording history of the traditional German techniques, lead to the publication in 1986 of *Willow Basketry of the Amana Colonies*. I wrote this book to share with others, as well as to preserve the information.

During my teaching experience, I realized the more simple willow basket techniques would help encourage students and expose them to a good experience with willow. That positive experience will lead students to go on to the more traditional willow basketry.

Some classes I teach: *Willow Weekend*, the third weekend in February; *Midwest Natural Basketmaking Seminar*, the last full weekend in April; *Association of Michigan Basketmaking Convention*, in October; as well as other locations across the U.S.

Inquiries are welcome regarding baskets of the area, classes and exhibits. See books by mail, page two.

GLOSSARY FOR THE VERY BEGINNER

Many words in this glossary are normal willow and basketweaving terms.
Several have been coined by the author to help students learn the basket techniques.

Back: Outside curve of a willow.

Bare bottom: Word coined to describe solid wood bottom of basket.

Base: Bottom of a basket.

Base border: Word coined to describe a willow border placed on the bottom (base) of a basket.

Belly: Inside curve of a willow.

Bi-stake or bye stake: Upright inserted alongside with an existing upright or inserted in weave separated from existing upright.

Bodkin: Tool that looks like a very fat awl. Used to make space for willows.

Border: Woven edge of a basket. Can be on top or bottom.

Bottom: Another name for the base of a basket.

Bow: Heavy willow used for handle center.

Brad point drill bit: Drill bit with very sharp pointed end.

Butt: Bottom thickest part of a willow.

Chase weave: Multiple sets of weavers following each other but never passing.

Crammed: Method of finishing off border uprights.

Enclosed: Word coined to describe a wooden base that is hidden.

Entwined: Word coined to describe two willows twisted into a handle.

Exposed: Word coined to describe a wooden base that shows.

Fake twisted handle: Coined term for a handle made out of reed rather than willow.

Four-rod wale. Willow technique using four weavers.

French randing: Willow weaving technique.

Pairing (Twining): Technique in which two weavers are used.

Pile-up: Coined word to describe fast French randing willows at beginning row.

Pound: Hitting weavers with a heavy object to tighten weave or level weave.

Pre-bend: Physically bending willow where you need it to bend.

Prick-up: Using knife, bodkin, or awl; to pre-bend upright so that it will not crack when bent up.

Rapping iron: Tool used to pound weavers to level basket. Anything heavy that fits between uprights will do the job.

Removable bottom rim: Foot added to basket bottom before handles are woven. Protects the base from wear and tear of everyday use. Rim wears and can be removed and replaced with new woven rim.

Round oval: Using a round circle stretched to make an oval shape, as opposed to a true oval which is "egg" shaped.

Row: One time around the diameter of the basket.

Scarf: Scraping the skin off the willow.

Self-handle: Coined word for handle opening in side of basket.

Shaker tape: Purchased weaving material.

Slype: Slant cut (English willow term).

GLOSSARY *continued*

GLOSSARY *continued*

Spacer: Piece of willow or other material that temporarily takes up space, and is replaced with real piece.

Splice: Where you end one willow and begin new willow.

Spokes: Framework of basket base or sides.

Swinger: Word coined to describe border weaver that weaves in front of other weavers.

Three-rod wale: Willow technique using three weavers.

Timber: Word coined to describe what an upright does when it borders down.

Tip: Top thin part of a willow.

Turndown: Timbering the uprights into a border.

Twining: Technique in which two weavers are used.

Twine-down: Twining on base with weavers hanging down bottom of base.

Twine-up: Twining on base with weavers woven up on top of base.

Upright: Stakes on the side of a basket.

Upsett or Upsetting: Pre-bending uprights up.

Woven base: Basket base that is woven.

Wrapper: Word coined to describe the willow around the handle bow.

TOOLS

Left to right:

Shoestring: To tie uprights for help in shaping.

Round fat screwdriver: Can be used when you do not have bodkin to make space for willow.

Pounding stick: To level rows and tighten weave (any round, heavy piece of wood is suitable).

Clip clothespin: To mark place you begin weaving if needed.

Fat round awl: Used when you do not have a bodkin to make space for a willow.

Pocketknife: Can be used a variety of ways. Not necessary if you have a fat round awl or screwdriver.

Pruning shears: Used to cut willow. Good sharp "Basket Scissors" will also work.

Work board: Thick 14-inch square plywood with hole to spike woven base down for working. Note: (photo above) hole in center of work board to spike down basket for working.

Tools not pictured:

Willow brake: Two smooth metal rods sprung together. Willow rod is drawn through to peel willow.

Five-gallon bucket for wild willows
55-gallon drum for cultured willows

The author, Joanna Schanz, has made a basket with only the "Basket Scissors" and a bodkin when other tools were not available.

Brief Information on Willows

CULTURED WILLOWS

All willows have a tip, back, belly, and butt.

To the best of our knowledge, the willow originally cultured in the Amana Colonies was the *Salix Nigra* (one of the black varieties). This is the cultured willow used today.

PLANTING AND CARE— The butt end of a willow is cut about twelve inches long and planted with a couple of eyes pointing upward. Position four willow cuttings in an eighteen-inch square with a fifth willow cutting in the center of the square.

The willows will be forced to grow up and straight. Cuttings can be planted in the fall, but you may have better luck planting in the early spring. Because cultured willows do not send out roots, where you plant your cutting is where your cultured willow bush will be.

The ground should be well-cultivated and kept weeded the first three years. Watering during drought periods is necessary until the patch is well established. Mulching is helpful to those of us who have limited garden time or patience. By the third year, your patch should be producing enough for basketmaking.

CUTTING—Cut your cultured willows after a killing frost when the leaves have fallen off and before the spring buds appear. No sap is running at this time, and you will not harm your cultured willow patch. Cut each branch, leaving a couple of eyes for next year's growth. Lay the willow butt ends together in a pile, ready to sort.

SORTING—Gather a big armful of willows and place butt ends into a container tall enough to hold the willows. Usually a 55-gallon drum or barrel is needed for the tall cultured willows. Shake the willows down so that all the butt ends are at the bottom of the barrel. Gently gather at the top and pull out only the tallest willows. Place these willows on a pile. Shake down the willows again and pull out the tallest ones. Put these either on the same pile as the first willows or start a new pile if the willows are noticeably shorter. Continue shaking down, gathering, pulling out the tallest, and piling until you have sorted all the willows. Sort by length, not thickness. Tie up your sorted willows and store until ready to use.

STORING—Store away from the sun, heat, and wind, any of which will dry the willows. The north side of a building, providing protection from the sun and wind, is a good place for storing covered willows. Inside an unheated building away from windows is another possibility, as are your freezer or root cellar. If willows become frozen, they can be thawed and used. If your willows should dry out, they can be soaked and used.

SOAKING—Soak for one to twelve days, depending on the thickness and the dryness. Any container that you can fit your willows into is usable. Stock tanks, children's wading pools, bathtubs, or a nearby creek are all good places. Willows float, so they need to be weighted down.

Count and select the willows you want to use and soak only those willows. Repeated soaking and drying of willows may discolor or weaken them.

SELECTING—Carefully select the willows you plan to use in a basket. Place the sorted willow piles on the ground. Look through the center of the pile to select willows for the

(Continued)

thickness you want to use for each step. To allow for broken willows, select several more than you think you will be using.

WILD WILLOWS

When cultured willows are not available, or for your first "learning" baskets while your cultured patch is growing, wild willows can be used with good results. Wild willow is not as strong as the cultured willow because it will not have as much wood.

WHERE TO FIND—Look for the bush willow, not the weeping willow tree. Look along river banks, on sand bars, in moist road ditches, and low-lying farm fields. Wild willow likes moisture and sun.

Spring and summer willow will be green and will be budding or have leaves. Fall willows will be reddish and may or may not have leaves. Winter willows are the easiest to locate because their reddish color stands out from the snow-white background.

A patch may look good from the road, but when you walk up to the patch, it may turn out to be old and overgrown. The ideal wild willow patch is one with a lot of one-year growth coming up out of the ground. Wild willow sends roots upward, and these roots spread.

When you locate a good usable patch, always get permission from the landowner and cut correctly so that you will be welcome to come back. A nice "thank you" to the landowner is one of your baskets.

CUTTING—Wild willow can be cut any time of year, except during the months of May through September. It is hard to kill a wild willow patch. Be sure you know the hazards before you go out to cut.

Cut the long slender willows. Stop at one willow bush and cut all the usable willows by following the willow from the tip end to the butt end, leaving eyes for next year. Cut nothing fatter than a pencil. After you have cut all the usable willows from one bush and

piled butt ends together, cut down the fat unusable willows and poke them back into the ground to re-root. Next year when you come back to the patch, you will have more to pick. Tie your usable willows in bundles that you can handle and take home to sort.

SORTING—Place one of your tied wild willow bundles in a five-gallon bucket and cut the tie off. Shake down the willows so that all the butt ends are at the bottom of the bucket. Gently gather at the top and pull out only the tallest willows. Place in a pile. Shake down again and pull out the tallest ones. Place these either on the same pile with the first group or start a new pile if the willows are noticeably shorter. Continue to shake down, gather, pull out the tall ones, and pile until you have sorted all the willows. Sort by length, not thickness. Tie your sorted piles and store till they are used.

STORING—The storing rules for cultured and wild willow are the same. Store away from the sun, heat, and wind, which are drying to willows. The north side of a building, providing protection from the sun and wind, is a good place for storing covered willows. Inside an unheated building away from sunlight is also a good storage place. Forgotten green willows stored and left unstirred will tend to mold, change color, and soften. Periodically stir green willows until completely dry to prevent molding. When your willows dry out, they can be soaked and used.

(Continued)

(Wild Willows continued)

SOAKING—When soaking wild willow, be sure that there are absolutely no leaves or foliage on the stems to spoil your water. Strip all the leaves off before soaking. Soaking time will depend on the dryness and thickness. Soak as you would cultured willows.

SELECTING—Before soaking, always select the willows you want to put into your basket. With the wild willow you will be using what you have picked from nature, and that may add character to your basket. You will find it helpful to look through the middle of your sorted piles for the thickness you need. You can spot a variety of thicknesses.

HAZARDS—Enjoy nature as you work in the wild willow patch, but, along with the quiet, peace, and earthy smells, you should be aware of some of the hazards.

Early morning and dusk are animal times. The scent of skunks has been noted, although this author has not yet seen one. Deer, raccoon, and rabbit leave their droppings behind to be stepped in, knelt on, and sat in. Snakes have been spotted sunning themselves from tops of willow bushes. When the willow patch is partially in water, splashes have been heard, but this author has not stayed around to find out what did the splashing.

When it is the hunting season, do not go hunting for willows. If you must go, dress like a hunter so you will not be mistaken for a deer. Expect the unexpected and do not forget that you are in nature's domain. Go with a friend, or be sure someone knows where you are going and when you will be returning.

PEELING WILLOWS

We have found several ways to successfully peel the skin off willows to make white willows. White willows tend to dry out fast after they have been peeled and usually have to be soaked before using.

BOILING—Willows can be softened by coiling into a large canner and boiling. How long to boil depends on the thickness of your willow (average is eight hours). After boiling, let willows soak in the water until they cool down. Color may be buff. Peel and store for later use.

PEELING BY HAND WHEN THE SAP IS RUNNING—By checking the willow patch each day in the early spring or fall, you can catch the willow when the sap is running up or down. The skin will peel off very easily. Start at the butt end, make three strips, and pull down to the tip. A willow brake tool will save time, but may damage the willow.

PEELING BY HAND WHEN THERE IS NO SAP RUNNING—Scrape the skin with a pocketknife, starting from the butt end.

PITTING—Stand bundles of sorted fresh willows in six inches of water. In the spring when the sap starts to rise, the willow can be easily peeled by hand or with a willow brake.

WILLOW SOURCES
Also sells willow slips to plant.

American Willow Growers Network*
Bonnie Gale (607) 847-8264
RFD #1 Box 124A
South New Berlin, NY 13843

Walters Ltd*
(414) 847-2276
Mountain Road
Washington Island, WI 54246

Pacific Weave
1-800-87-WEAVE
3008-B 16th Avenue West
Seattle, WA 98119

Willowglen Nursery*
Lee Zieke (319) 735-5570
3512 Lost Mile Road
Decorah, IA 52101

Whale-Inn Farms*
Sandra Whalen (313) 685-2459
800 Moore Road
Milford, MI 48381

The Caning Shop
(415) 527-5010
926 Gilman Street at 8th
Berkeley, CA 94710

BASKETRY STEPS

WOVEN BASE

Base Spokes
Twine Base
Insert Uprights and Upsett
Sideweaving
    Four-Rod Wale
    French Randing
Border Timbered

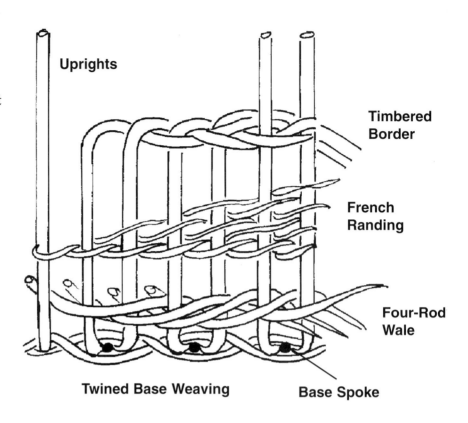

Uprights

Timbered Border

French Randing

Four-Rod Wale

Twined Base Weaving

Base Spoke

WOODEN BASE

Prepare Wood Base
Insert Uprights
Sideweaving
    Three-Rod Wale
    French Randing
Border Crammed

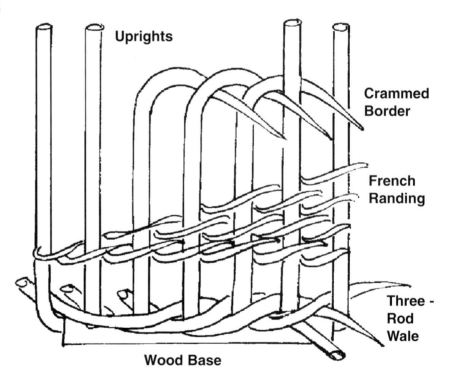

Uprights

Crammed Border

French Randing

Three-Rod Wale

Wood Base

WOODEN BASE

EXPOSED:

Preparation of wooden base:

1. Use 3/8 to 1/2 inch thick solid wood board cut to desired size and shape.

2. Mark holes 1 1/4 inches apart, center to center. Size of holes should be larger than the willow butts you will be using so that the willow inserts easily, but does not scarf the skin (if using barked willow), or squash the willow (if using peeled willow).

3. If using a handle, you should make certain your drilled holes will accommodate your handle. Two general rules: one hole for wrapped handle; two holes for wooden handle between the uprights.

Inserting uprights/turning down butt border:

1. Base border/turn down will be on the bottom of wooden base. You will do a simple turn down with the butts on the bottom of base before weaving on the sides. Tips should be on top, butts on bottom.

2. Insert three upright butts. Turn down first butt/upright outside one, inside one. You can put a spacer between the wooden base and first butt/upright to help make space for the last butt/upright when you end the butt bottom border (see diagram I).

3. Insert another butt/upright. Turn down the second butt/upright, outside one, inside one (See diagram II). Continue inserting a butt/upright and turning down a butt/upright until you are back to the beginning. The last butt/upright goes outside one (the first butt/upright) then inside one, resting on the inside of the second butt/upright (see diagram III). Last butt/upright replaces the spacer.

4. Trim.

5. Turn basket right side up. Put a weight in wooden bottom for stability (diagram IV).

6. You are ready for sideweaving.

I. Inserting uprights/turning down butt border:

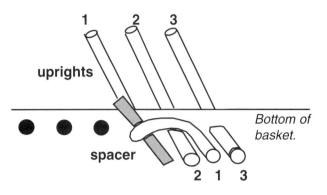

II. Inserting uprights:

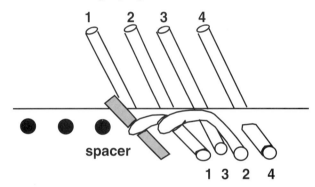

III. Last upright replaces spacer:

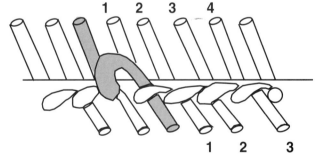

IV.

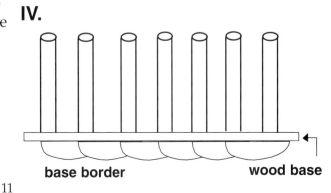

ENCLOSED:

Preparation of wooden base:

1. Plywood can be used because the base will not show on the sides of the basket. Use 1/4-inch plywood, cut to the size of the desired base and shape. Mark holes 1 to 1 1/4 inches apart, center to center. Holes should be slightly larger than the willows you will be using so butts can be inserted easily and not scarf the bark, (if using barked willow), or squash the willow (if using peeled willow).

2. If using a handle, plan where your handle will be to make sure your drilled holes will accommodate your handle. One hole for a willow-pegged or a wrapped handle. Two holes are needed for a wooden handle to go between the two uprights.

Inserting uprights and turning down butts:

1. You will do a simple turndown.

2. Insert butts of willow up from the bottom of the base. The turn down will be in the inside of your basket bottom.

3. Insert three butts. Turn down first butt by weaving inside one—towards center; outside one—towards outside edge of wooden base (see diagram I). You can put a spacer under the first butt between the wooden base and first butt, after it makes its move.

4. Insert another butt. Turn down the second butt inside one, outside one (diagram II). Continue to insert new butts and turn down next in line butts. The last butt will go inside one (the first butt timbered) and under the first butt where the spacer is placed (diagram III). Remove the spacer.

5. Trim at edge of wood base (see shaded area of uprights in diagram III).

Upsetting uprights:

1. Each upright is to be rolled over an awl or bodkin placed between the wooden base and upright to the outside of the wood base (see diagram IV).

2. Tie up. You are ready for sideweaving.

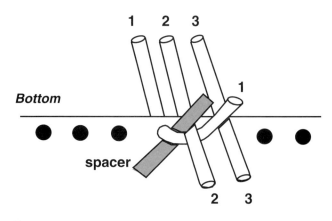

I. **Inserting upright** *View: inside of basket*

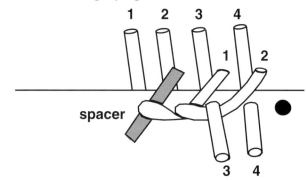

II. **Inserting upright**

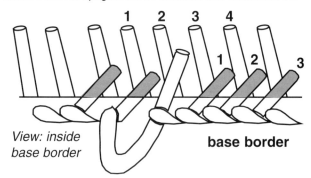

III. **Last upright replaces spacer**

Shaded area of uprights will be trimmed. See instruction #5.

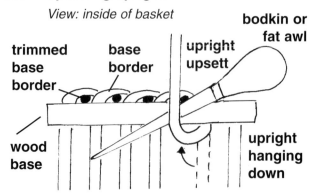

IV. **Upsetting uprights**

View: inside of basket

12

BARE BOTTOM

Preparation of wooden base:

1. You start with a 3/4 to 7/8 inch thick solid wood base, cut to the desired size and shape.

2. Mark holes 3/4 to 2 inches apart on the edge of the wooden base. The distance between holes is determined by size of base and whether you are using a mold.

3. Holes can be closer together if using a brad point bit. Drill holes the exact size of the willow uprights. The size of the holes should average 17/64 inch or 1/4 inch. Placing the wooden base in a vise helps drill straight down 3/4 to 1 inch deep. If holes are too large, the willow butts will not stay in place. If holes are too small, you can cut off the fat of a butt. You do not want to cut so much that your upright becomes too short or too thin.

Inserting uprights:

1. Place the base bottom on a work board where you have plenty of room. A stool or swivel piano stool works great. If using a mold, attach the wooden base to the mold, bottom-side up. Insert willow butt ends of uprights in holes with back of willow to the outside and belly of the willow towards the inside of your basket (see diagrams I-II).

2. Turn base right-side up. Push the upright in the hole before you prick up (pre-bend) upright 1/4 inch from wood base (see diagram III). Gather up and tie. The 1/4 inch leaves room for your first row of weaving for your base border (see diagram IV).

3. You are ready for sideweaving.

Inserting uprights:

I. Wooden base placed on table.

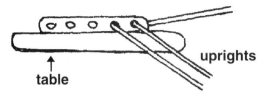

uprights

table

II. Wooden base attached on to a mold.

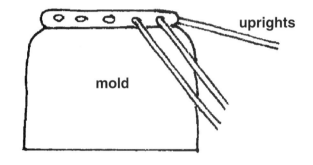

uprights

mold

III. 1/4 space between wood and bent-up place.

space

IV.

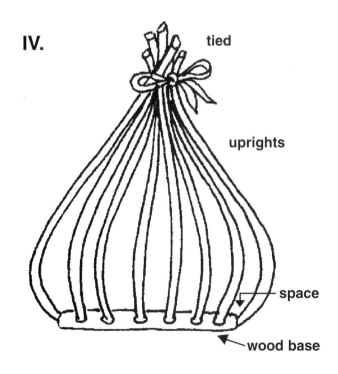

tied

uprights

space

wood base

13

WOVEN BASE

ROUND 3/3 WOVEN BASE

Base spokes (three spokes inside of three)

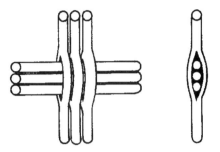

1. Cut six fat butt ends two inches longer than desired base diameter. Insert three base spokes inside three base spokes, alternating heavy and thinner ends (see diagram I).

2. Using two tips, begin twining down (with weavers hanging down) between three to tie or hold base beginning together (see diagram II).

3. After two or three rows, begin twining between each base spoke, spreading spokes evenly apart. The sooner you can get the base spokes spread evenly, the neater your base will be. Be sure you move the base spoke where it needs to be and weave around the spoke. Do not just weave (see diagram III).

4. When weaver becomes too fat or too short, splice butts (see diagram below) and continue to weave. Splicing both weavers at the same time makes a neater base. Continue twining and splicing tip to tip and butt to butt. Try not to have splices on the same base spoke or side of the base each time you splice.

5. When you reach the desired diameter for your base, end with the tips. Tuck each tip end into previous row of weaving.

6. Trim.

7. Ready for uprights and sideweaving.

II. **Twining over four sets of base spokes**

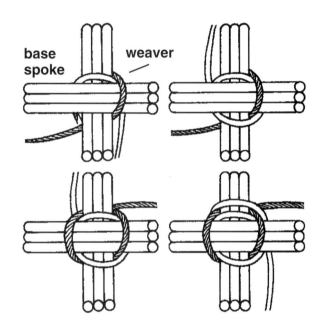

III. **Twining between each base spoke**

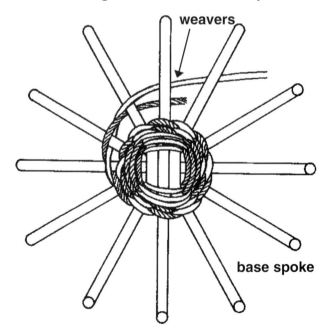

Correct splice

Incorrect splice

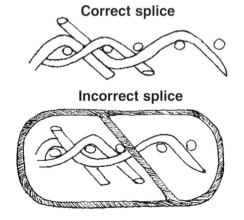

ROUND 4/4 WOVEN BASE

1. Cut eight fat base spokes two inches longer than desired diameter.

2. Insert four base spokes inside four spokes (see diagram I).

3. Beginning with two tips, twine between four spokes to tie base spokes together (see diagram II on page 14).

4. After two or three rows, twine between two spokes for a couple rows (see diagram II), then twine between individual spokes, spreading evenly (see diagram III). The sooner you can get the base spokes evenly spaced, the neater your base will be.

5. Be sure you move the base spoke where it needs to be, and weave around the spoke with the weaver. Do not just weave.

6. When weaver becomes too fat or too short, splice butts (see diagram below) and continue to weave. Splice both weavers at the same time but do not splice on the same base spoke twice in a row.

7. Continue twining, splicing butt to butt, and tip to tip.

8. End with tips at desired diameter, tuck tips in previous row.

Splicing diagrams also provided on page 14.

Correct splice

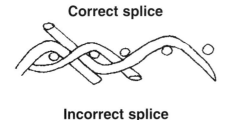

Incorrect splice

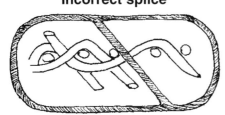

I. Base spokes (four inside of four)

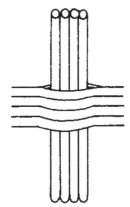

II. Twining between two base spokes

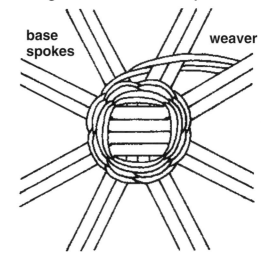

base spokes

weaver

III. Twining between individual base spokes

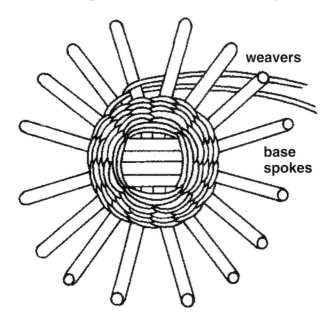

weavers

base spokes

OVAL: 3/5 WOVEN BASE

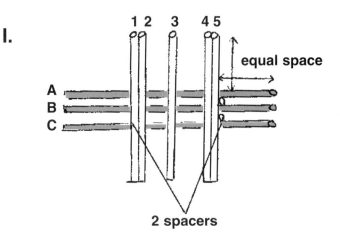

I.

1. Three/five: Cut three fat base spokes two inches longer than the desired length of the oval base (A, B, C). Cut five fatter base spokes two inches longer than the desired width of the oval base (1, 2, 3, 4, 5).

2. Insert the three longer length base spokes (A, B, C) inside the five shorter width base spokes (1, 2, 3, 4, 5). Arrange as shown in the diagram with two spacers (see diagram I).

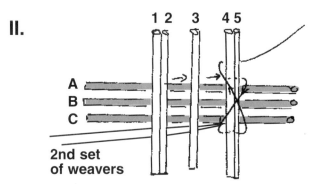

II.

3. Base Twining: You will be twining with two sets of weavers so your oval base will be balanced and neat. Beginning with two tips inserted in the crack alongside the length base spoke, weave with one of the weavers diagonal across the two width spokes (4, 5). Under the spokes, diagonal back to form an "X" on the top side of the end-width spokes (see diagram II). Pick up second weaver in the set and diagonal UNDER the two width spokes (4, 5). Over the spokes, diagonal back to form an "X" on the underside of the end width spokes (see diagram III). The "X" on each end helps keep the two end width spokes together before they need to be separated.

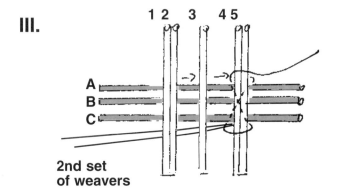

III.

4. Repeat direction #3, using the second set of weavers. "X" over and under spokes 1 and 2. Use the weavers to begin twining between the length spokes (A, B, C) of weavers (see diagram IV).

5. One set of weavers MUST NOT pass the other set of weavers When you come to the other set, drop the present set of weavers and weave with the new set of weavers (see diagram IV).

6. After two passes around the ends, twine between the two end width spokes, spreading them evenly.

OVAL: 3/5 WOVEN BASE *continued*

IV. Two sets of weavers: Twining and chasing but never passing.

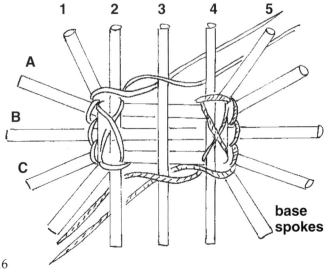

OVAL: 3/5 WOVEN BASE *continued*

7. After one row is twined between each spoke, you will begin switching to reverse twining each time you come to the middle spoke on the long side. This will create a "V" look to the rows. It will help to keep your oval willow base from twisting.

8. Reverse twining. DO NOT GO THE OPPOSITE DIRECTION. When weaving with the German willow method, you are twining-down when weaving a base (see diagram I). The English method of twining requires twining-up when weaving a base. When twining-down your weavers are hanging down from the base. When twining-up, your weavers are brought up with each stroke of twining on the top of the base (see diagram II). Reverse twining on a base is simply switching from up to down or down to up.

9. Splice butt to butt and tip to tip. Splice in a balanced way with each set of weavers spliced opposite the other set.

10. Continue weaving with the two sets of weavers doing twining and reverse twining until you have reached your desired oval base size, ending with tips tucked in the previous row.

11. Trim.

12. Ready for uprights and sideweaving.

I. Twining down

View: looking down into the base

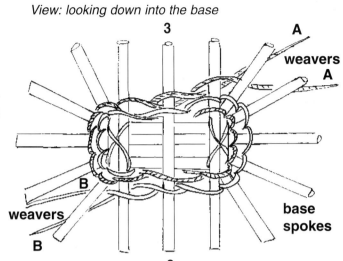

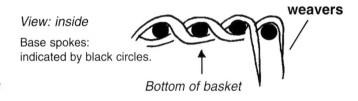

View: inside

Base spokes: indicated by black circles.

Bottom of basket

II. Twining up

View: looking down into the base

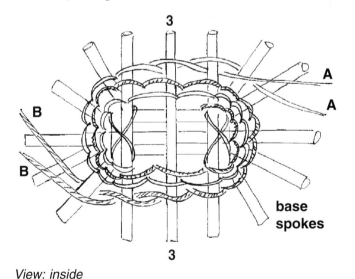

View: inside

Base spokes: indicated by black circles.

Bottom of basket

UPSETTING ON WOVEN BASE

ROUND

1. Usually you will have two uprights for each base spoke. A Three/Three base will have 24 uprights and a Four/Four base will have 32 uprights. Sometimes, recipes (patterns) will instruct to use a 1-2-1-2-1-2-etc., insertion for uprights. That means that every other base spoke gets only one upright.

2. Uprights should be heavier than your weavers and as evenly matched as possible. If you match up the thickness at the point of your turndown, then cut the butts, you can have a very balanced turndown (see diagram III).

3. Slype (cut diagonally) butts of willows and insert along each side of a base spoke. Use a fat awl or bodkin if you need to make space for the upright. This should be inserted at least one inch—a longer insert is better (see diagrams I and II).

4. When all have been inserted, prick up and tie in an orderly fashion.

I. Inserting uprights
View: looking down into the basket

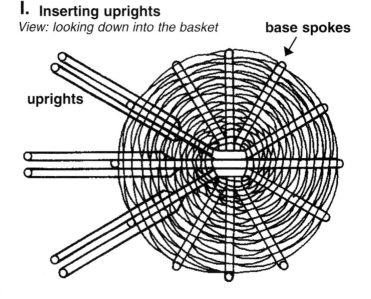

II. Inserting uprights
View: side

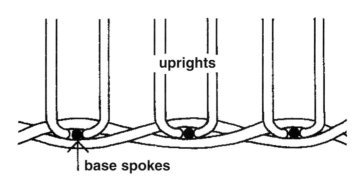

III.

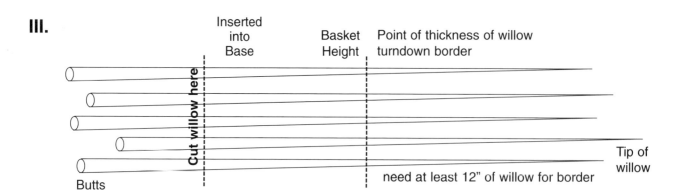

18

OVAL BASES

1. The number of uprights may vary. You need to have the spacing as evenly as possible. Consequently, not all base spokes will have two uprights. Rule of thumb: on a curved area of the base there should be two uprights per base spoke, and on the long side, use one upright per base spoke (see diagrams I and II).

2. Uprights should be heavier than your weavers and as evenly matched as possible. If you match up the thickness at the point of your turndown, then cut the butts, you can then have a very balanced turndown (see diagram III).

3. Slype butts of willows and insert along base spokes as instructed in the basket recipe (pattern). Use a fat awl or bodkin if you need to make space for the upright. This should be inserted at least one inch, although a longer insert is better.

4. After all uprights are inserted, prick up and tie in an orderly fashion.

5. You are ready for sideweaving.

I. *Base spokes are shaded.*

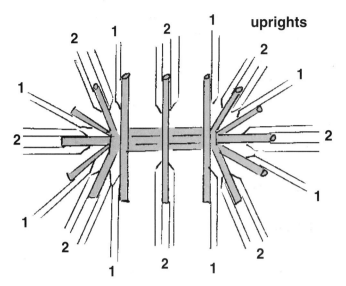

II.

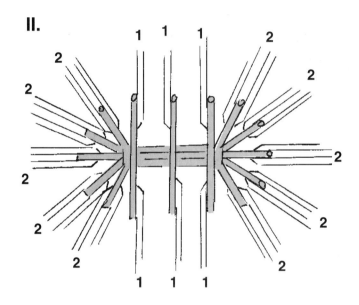

III.

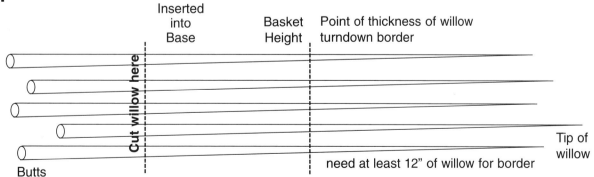

BASE BORDER

1. On an exposed base a base border is not necessary as the uprights inserted and timbered-down provide the base border.

2. On an enclosed base, the base border can be woven. However, a removable bottom rim looks and works better.

3. On a bare bottom, a base border can be used but it is not necessary as the wooden base rests on the floor. If a base border is used, be sure the base border does not hang below the wooden base (see diagram I-IV).

4. On a woven base, a base border is usually used if a removable bottom rim will not be used. There are a couple different base borders to use. The method depends upon what you want the base border to look like and the size of base.

I. Base Border on Bare Bottom
Weavers are shaded.

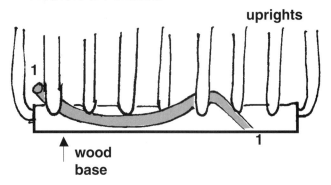

II.

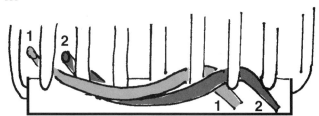

III.

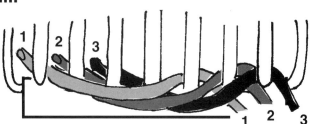

IV.

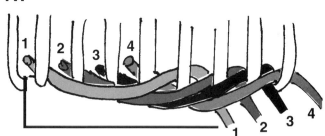

Three/One Base Border I

1. Insert four medium weavers behind four consecutive uprights beginning with butt, tip, butt, tip (see diagrams I-IV). Weave left weaver in front of three, behind one. Pull the weaver down as close to the base sides as possible. You may be able to wedge the weaver (see diagram V) between the upright and the base spoke.

2. Pick up the weaver on the left and weave 3-1 again pulling down so it is wedged. Continue weaving from the left 3-1 until back to the beginning. Match up the ends with beginning. You will always have four weavers wedged behind four consecutive uprights, if not, you have made a mistake in weaving. If you have, you should go backwards until you find where you did not pick up the left weaver or did not weave 3-1.

I.

Base spokes are indicated below by small black circles.

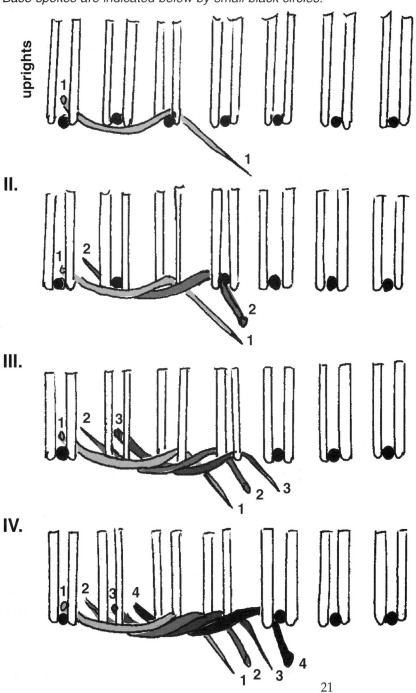

V. Wedge the weaver

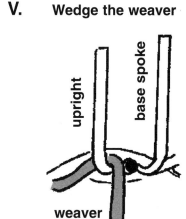

21

Three/One Base Border II

1. Select eight medium fat willows. Slype the butt ends of four and insert to the right of four consecutive base spokes or insert into the base to the right of the upright. Beginning with left weaver, weave in front of three, behind one and out. Wedge the weaver gently, but firmly, down between the upright and base spoke.

2. Continue weaving 3-1 halfway around the basket. Drop the first set of weavers and insert a second set of four slyped butt ends. Continue with the second set of weavers.

3. **There are two ways to continue:**
   a. First method is to match the last weavers with the first weavers and stop weaving. Trim. You are ready for sideweaving (see diagrams I & II).
   b. The second method is to match the weaver with the first butt beginning, pull down and drop. With the other three weavers left, continue to weave 3-1 one more stroke. These three continue to be used, weaving a three-rod wale which is in front of two, behind one and out (see diagrams III-VI).

Base Border I & II Ending

Matching ending with beginning.
Uprights below are indicated by black circles.

I.

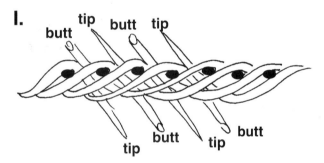

II.

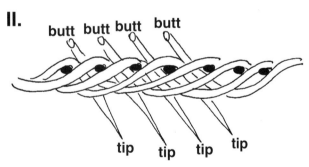

III. Base Border Continue Weaving
(three-rod wale)

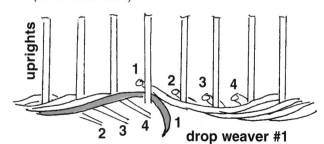

drop weaver #1

IV. Continue to weave 2nd weaver

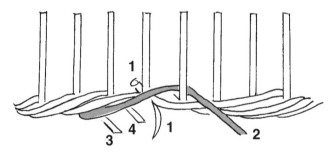

V. Continue to weave 3rd weaver

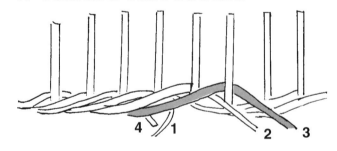

VI. Continue to weave 4th weaver

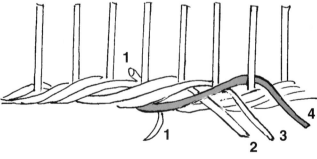

Weavers 2, 3, and 4, now weave three-rod wale.

SHAPING

1. Molds and forms are great but not always available.

2. Wooden round and oval hoops are very helpful but need to be attached to uprights. The willow uprights can still lean one way or the other.

3. A tie on top was used in the old Amana Colony basketry to help control uprights. That is the method Philip taught me. A tie on top is very helpful when uprights are long enough to let the tie do its job. Uprights need to be gathered in an orderly fashion so the tie will slide up or down. Moving the tie up, flares the sides, and moving the tie down, brings the sides in towards the center.

4. Using two ties (see diagram I), with the second one higher than the controlling tie, helps keep the controlling tie in place. When the top tie flies off the uprights, you know the controlling tie will soon follow. This is the time to regroup and check out what is happening to your shape.

5. My rule for shaping "helpers" is: there are no rules. Whatever you find to help you can be used. Using a round weight from a weight set is very useful (see diagram II). The weights have a hole in the center so you can spike your basket to a work surface. They are heavy for good base stability and allow your eyes to see a round shape to help you control the round shape.

SHAPING *continued*

I.

Two ties.

II.

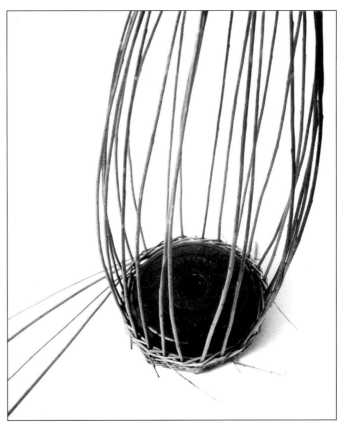

Round weight in a round basket helps to keep the shape of the basket.

SHAPING continued

6. After each two or three rows, pound down the weaving. When you pound, the tie usually moves. Hold the tie in place when pounding. Pound and level with ruler between each step of weaving sides.

5. All shaping "helpers" still need the weaver to pay close attention to the uprights and their position. ALWAYS REMEMBER: Hold uprights where you want them and weave around upright to hold in proper place. This takes practice. As you develop the habit of weaving around uprights it becomes easier. Do not just weave letting the weaver determine the shape. Use your hands, thumbs, and fingers. Look at the uprights you are weaving around. How is the space between uprights? Is it even? Are the uprights lined up for the shape you want? When you stop to pound down the weaving, also check your shape, the tie, and look at your basket from a distance (see diagrams III-IV).

8. Do not get discouraged if your first willow basket is not the shape you wanted. It takes practice and remember this rule: Put the upright where you want it to be and weave around it with the weaver.

III.

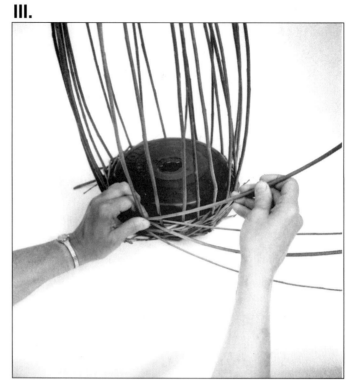

Using thumb and index finger, pinch weaver and upright to hold upright in correct position. Keeps weaver from pushing upright towards the inside of the basket.

IV.

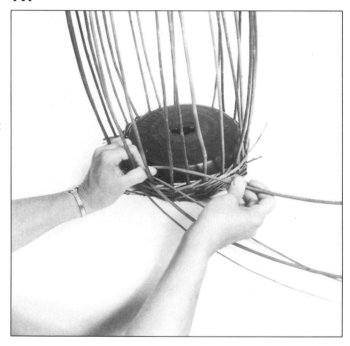

Using thumb to guide weaver behind the upright so that the weaver does not push upright out of proper position.

SIDEWEAVING

THREE-ROD WALE

1. Select three willow weavers that are skinnier or more flexible than your uprights. Insert three weavers behind three consecutive uprights. Begin with the weaver on the left and weave in front of two, behind one and out. Notice you still have three weavers coming out from behind three consecutive uprights. Pick up weaver on the left and weave 2-1. Continue to pick up and weave 2-1. You will always have three weavers in a row. If not, unweave to see what went wrong (see diagrams I-II).

2. There are three ways to begin a three-rod wale. Begin with all three tips, all three butt ends, or alternately butt, tip, butt.

3. Splicing is usually butt to butt and tip to tip unless a specific basket recipe says differently. Splice side-to-side with a new weaver behind the old weaver, NOT the new weaver on top of the old one. You want the splice to be one row in height and not look like two rows from the side or create a space (see diagram III, seen also on pages 14 and 15). When all three weavers have passed their beginning point, you have completed one row.

4. After weaving a couple rows, pound down the weaving to compensate for any shrinkage and to level your basket. Check your shape and re-tie if necessary.

I. Three-rod wale
Uprights indicated below by black circles.

II. Three-rod wale

III. Correct splice

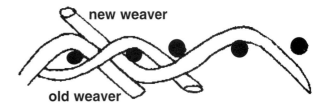

Incorrect splice

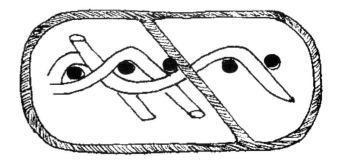

FOUR-ROD WALE: TWO-TWO

1. Select four willow weavers that are skinnier or more flexible than your uprights. Insert four weavers behind four consecutive uprights. Begin with the weaver on the left and weave in front of two, behind two and out. Notice you still have four weavers coming out from behind four consecutive uprights. Pick up weaver on the left and weave 2-2. Continue to pick up and weave 2-2. You will always have four weavers in a row. If not, unweave to see what went wrong (see diagrams I-II).

2. There are three ways to begin four-rod wale. Begin with all tips, all butt ends, or alternately butt, tip, butt, tip.

3. Splicing is usually butt to butt and tip to tip unless a specific basket recipe says differently. Splice side-to-side with a new weaver behind old weaver, not the new weaver on top of the old one. You want the splice to be one row in height and not look like two rows from the side or to create a space. When all four weavers have passed their beginning point, you have completed one row.

4. After weaving a couple of rows, pound down the weaving to compensate for any shrinkage and to level your basket.

5. Check your shape and re-tie if necessary.

I. Four-rod wale inserted

Uprights are indicated by black circles.

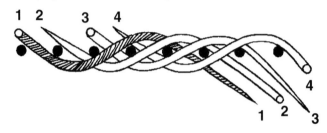

II. Four-rod wale weaving

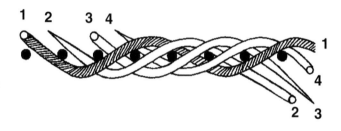

FOUR-ROD WALE: THREE-ONE

1. Four-rod wale woven 3-1 is the same as 2-2 except you will be weaving the left weaver in front of three, behind one and out. The four-rod wale 3-1 creates a nice ridge around the basket when woven for one row only. Also four-rod wale 3-1 is used for most base borders (see diagrams I-II).

I. Four-rod wale 3-1 inserted

Uprights are indicated by black circles.

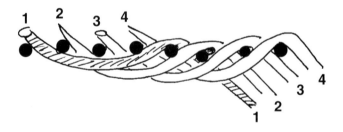

II. Four-rod wale 3-1 weaving

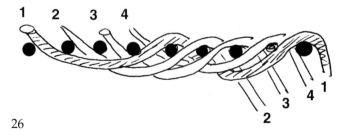

FRENCH RANDING

French Randing is a very fast weave but it is not as strong as a three-rod wale or four-rod wale. Until a student understands that French randing moves diagonally up the side of a basket, it may be difficult. However, when teaching willow over a mold, I noticed that very few students got confused when "unpiling" or "cleaning out the basement." When working on a mold, you are holding the basket at a different angle than when you are working on a table. You are looking at the weaving bottom side up and it is easy to see which willows in French randing are to weave. It is easy to see that the weavers each take a turn. If you have a difficult time in the beginning when learning French randing, sit lower than your basket so you are looking at the weave bottom side up.

NOTES

1-1 BEGINNING

Inserting French Randing

1. Select French randing weavers equal to the number of uprights you have. All French randing weavers should be the same thickness and length. You will be inserting all French randing weavers before you begin to weave row by row. Butt ends are always inserted unless a basket recipe says to insert tip end.

2. Insert the first French randing weaver behind one upright and weave in front of one, behind one and out. Insert the second French randing weaver behind the upright TO THE LEFT of the first upright. Weave in front of one, behind one and out. Insert the next upright, weave in front of one, behind one, and out. Continue to insert the French randing weavers behind the upright to the left until all French randing weavers have been inserted (see diagram I).

3. CAUTION: The last French randing weavers will have to be inserted under the first French randing weavers and weave under the first French randing weavers. When completed, check to be sure each upright has a weaver coming out on top of another (see diagram II).

4. When weaving French randing, you are inserting to the left, but the willows will still flow downstream.

Weaving rows

1. After all French randing weavers are inserted and checked to make sure the pattern is correct, you can begin weaving each row. Choose any weaver to begin. Weave in front of one, behind one and out. Drop that weaver and pick up the next weaver ON THE LEFT of the first weaver and weave 1-1 (see diagram I on page 30). You will be weaving each weaver ON THE LEFT 1-1 until all weavers have had a turn.

2. CAUTION: The first and second French randing of the row will be on top of the last two French randings of the row (also called "the pile-up"). When you come to the end BE SURE TO weave the last weavers which are the two on the bottom of "the pile-up" 1-1. The last two weavers must NOT cross over the first weavers of the row. Think of the last weavers taking their turn playing "follow the leader," coming up out of "the pile up." They do not play "leap frog," jumping up on top of the weavers from the beginning of the row.

3. To weave next row, pick any weaver to begin and weave 1-1. Moving to your left, weave 1-1, remembering that these first two will be on top of your last two of the row in "the pile-up." Continue weaving 1-1 until you are back to only one weaver coming from behind one upright, with no weaver jumping up on top of the beginning.

4. You are done weaving French randing when you have reached the tips and have no more willow to weave.

I. *The uprights are indicated by black circles in the following two diagrams.*

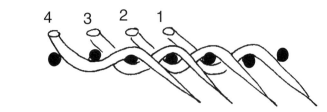

II.

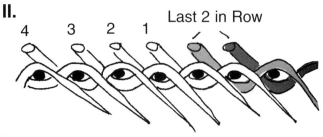

28

2-1 BEGINNING

Inserting French Randing

1. Select French randing weavers equal to the number of uprights you have. All French randing weavers should be the same thickness and length. You will be inserting all French randing weavers before you begin to weave row by row. Butt ends are always inserted unless a basket recipe says to insert tip end.

2. Insert the first French randing weaver behind one upright and weave in front of two, behind one and out. Insert the second French randing weaver behind the upright TO THE LEFT of the first upright. Weave in front of two, behind one and out. Insert the second upright, weave in front of two, behind one, and out. Continue to insert the French randing weavers behind the upright to the left until all French randing weavers have been inserted (see diagram I).

3. CAUTION: the last French randing weavers will have to be inserted under the first French randing weavers and weave under the first French randing weavers. When completed, check to be sure each upright has a weaver coming out on top of another (see diagram II).

4. When weaving French randing, you are inserting to the left, but the willows will still flow downstream.

Weaving rows

1. After all French randing weavers are inserted and checked to make sure the pattern is correct, you can begin weaving each row. Choose any weaver to begin. Weave in front of one, behind one and out. Drop that weaver and pick up the next weaver ON THE LEFT of the first weaver and weave 1-1 (see diagram I on page 30). You will be weaving each weaver ON THE LEFT 1-1 until all weavers have had a turn.

The uprights are indicated by black circles in the following two diagrams.

I. Inserting French randing (beginning)

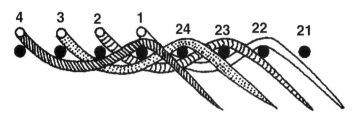

II. Inserting the last French randing weavers

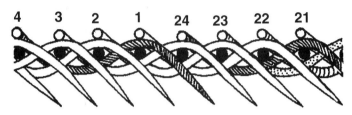

2. CAUTION: The first and second French randing of the row will be on top of the last two French randing of the row (also called "the pile-up"). When you come to the end BE SURE TO weave the last weavers which are the two on the bottom of "the pile-up" 1-1. The last two weavers must NOT cross over the first weavers of the row. Think of the last weavers taking their turn playing "follow the leader," coming up out of "the pile-up." They do not play "leap frog," jumping up on top of the weavers from the beginning of the row.

3. To weave next row, pick any weaver to begin and weave 1-1. Moving to your left, weave 1-1, remembering that these first two will be on top of your last two of the row in "the pile-up." Continue weaving 1-1 until you are back to only one weaver coming from behind one upright, with no weaver jumping up on top of the beginning.

4. You are done weaving French randing when you have reached the tips and have no more willow to weave.

FAST FRENCH RANDING

Once you understand the technique of French randing, you can weave French randing fast.

1. Insert all French randing weavers (one per upright).

2. You will be weaving three rows at once. Don't panic. Weave first weaver 1-1. Weave second weaver 1-1 (see diagram I). Weave third weaver 1-1 twice (third weaver will be on top of first weaver, creating a pile-up. Weave fourth weaver 1-1 twice—again adding to the pile-up (see diagram II). Weave fifth weaver 1-1 three times—adding to the pile-up. Weave sixth weaver 1-1 three times—adding to the pile-up (see diagram III). You will now have two pile-ups with four weavers. The bottom weavers are the last ones in your line up.

FAST FRENCH RANDING continued

I.   1st weaver 1-1; 2nd weaver 1-1

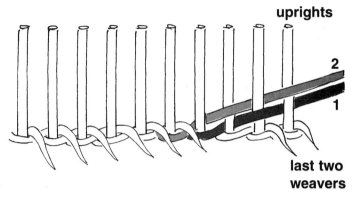

uprights

last two weavers

II.   3rd weaver 1-1 twice
4th weaver 1-1 twice;

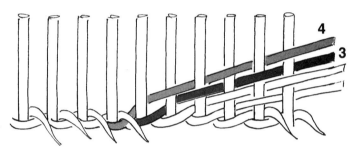

III.   5th weaver 1-1 three times
6th weaver 1-1 three times

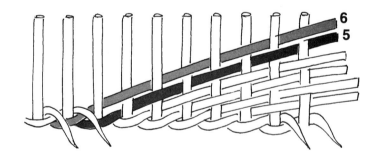

FAST FRENCH RANDING *continued*

3. The rest of the weavers take their turn weaving 1-1 three times, but do not add to pile-up until you get to the end (the pile-up) where you go backwards or "clean out the basement" or "unpile" from the bottom up (see diagram IV-V).

Follow diagram V. for instructions 4-6.

4. The bottom (#1) of the pile weaves 1-1 three times. The second weaver (#2) on the bottom weaves 1-1 three times. You now have only three in each pile-up.

5. The bottom (#3) of the pile weaves 1-1 two times. The second weaver (#4) on the bottom weaves 1-1 two times. You now have only two in each pile-up.

6. The bottom (#5) of the pile weaves 1-1 one time. The second weaver (#6) on the bottom weaves 1-1 one time. You now should have your "basement all cleaned out" and no pile-up.

7. Pound down level. Weave another *Fast* French randing.

8. You are done weaving *Fast* French randing when you have reached the tips and have no more willow to weave.

9. Hint: If you come to the pile-up and do not know how many times to weave 1-1, count the number of weavers that are piled on top of the weaver. The number of weavers on top of the bottom weaver is the number of times you must weave 1-1. Also, you will be "cleaning out the basement" moving the weaver up and out to catch up with the other weavers but not pass those weavers.

IV. *Fast* French randing "pile-up"

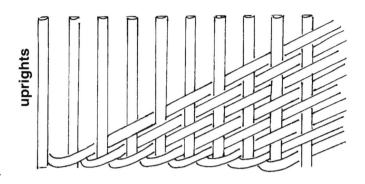

V. Cleaning out the Basement

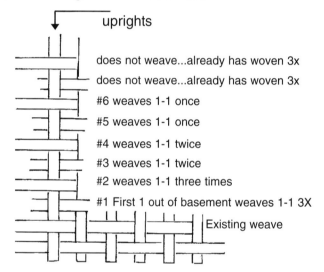

uprights

does not weave...already has woven 3x
does not weave...already has woven 3x
#6 weaves 1-1 once
#5 weaves 1-1 once
#4 weaves 1-1 twice
#3 weaves 1-1 twice
#2 weaves 1-1 three times
#1 First 1 out of basement weaves 1-1 3X
Existing weave

31

BORDERS

CRAMMED 1-2

1. Place a willow spacer the same size as the uprights to the right of the first upright you want to timber (turndown). This spacer will make space for the last upright (see diagram I).

2. Timber the first upright behind the second upright and out. Timber each succeeding upright behind and out. The last upright, when it timbers behind one and out, will replace the spacer you inserted at the very beginning (diagram II).

3. Each upright swings forward in front of two timbered uprights and is crammed in place. To cram, use your fingernail to bend the swinger down right where you want it to bend, slant cut 1 to 1 1/2 inches below the bend. Insert bent swinger along the side to the left of the third timbered upright. Continue to bend, snip, and tuck your way around the basket until all uprights are completed (see diagrams III-IV).

CRAMMED 1-3

1. Place a willow spacer the same size as the upright to the right of the first upright you want to timber (turndown). This spacer will make space for the last upright (see diagram V).

2. Timber the first upright behind the second upright and out. Timber each succeeding upright behind one and out. The last upright, when it timbers behind one and out, will replace the spacer you inserted at the very beginning (diagram VI).

3. Each upright now swings forward in front of three timbered uprights. Using your fingernail, bend the swinger where you need it to bend, slant cut 1 to 1 1/2 inches below bend and insert alongside the left of the fourth timbered upright. Continue to bend, snip and cram your way around the basket until all uprights are completed (see diagrams VII-VIII).

32

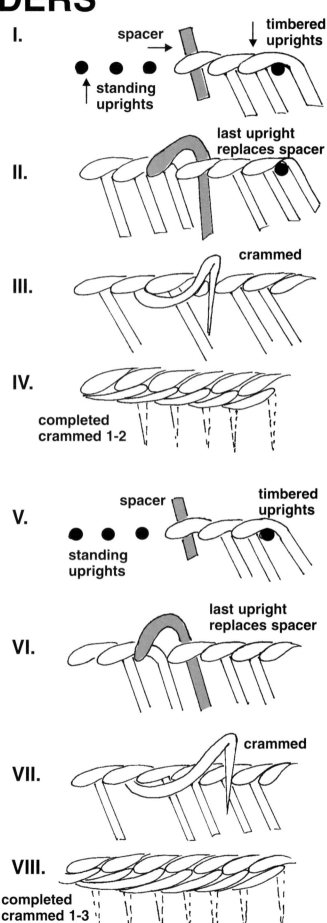

I. spacer → ↓ timbered uprights
↑ standing uprights

II. last upright replaces spacer

III. crammed

IV. completed crammed 1-2

V. spacer ← timbered uprights
standing uprights

VI. last upright replaces spacer

VII. crammed

VIII. completed crammed 1-3

CRAMMED *continued*

CRAMMED 2-3

1. Place a willow spacer the same size as the upright to the right of the first upright and the second upright you want to timber (turndown). These two spacers will make space for the last two uprights (see diagram IX).

2. Timber the first upright behind two and out. Timber each succeeding upright behind two and out. The last two uprights, when they timber behind two, will replace the two spacers you inserted one at a time (see diagram X).

3. Each upright swings forward in front of three timbered uprights. Using your fingernail, bend the swinger where it will be crammed along the left side of the fourth timbered upright. Slant cut 1 to 1 1/2 inches below the bend and insert alongside the third timbered upright. Continue to bend, snip, and cram your way around the basket until all uprights are completed (see diagrams XI-XII).

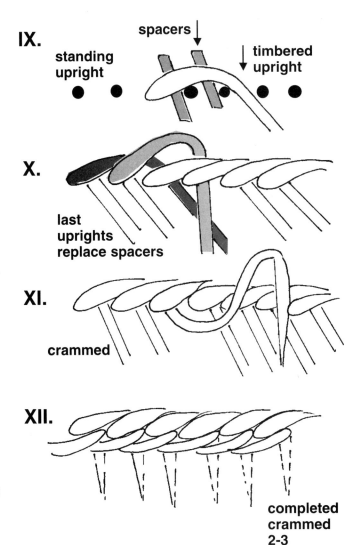

IX. spacers / standing upright / timbered upright

X. last uprights replace spacers

XI. crammed

XII. completed crammed 2-3

BORDER STORY

During one class, a student was having a terrible time remembering that the uprights count when you go in front of and behind, whether they are standing up or timbered. To help students remember to keep the swinger on the outside, we always used the story that the swinger is on the outside of the timbered willow because he is a gentleman protecting his date. A man used to walk on the outside next to the street as well as open doors for ladies. So, I just expanded on that theme:

"A swinger walks into a bar looking for a date. He swings in front of the first lady but she is down, passed out on the floor. He swings in front of the next lady who is standing upright and the swinger asks her out. The swinger goes behind the standing upright lady and out the door. The upright lady timbers and follows him out the door to join him. The swinging gentleman walks on the outside with his date (the timbered upright who is now a swinger)."

I don't think the student will ever forget to count the upright who fell off her stool and got passed by.

FOUR-ROD TURNDOWN 1-3 USING SPACERS

1. Each upright will timber behind one, swing in front of three, behind one, and out. After an upright timbers it becomes a swinger.

2. Pre-bend the first upright because you will need space near the end of your border to thread a willow through. (See diagram I below.)

3. Timber the first upright behind one and out. Place a spacer the same thickness as the upright to the front of the timbered upright (see diagram II).

4. Do the same with three more consecutive uprights for a total of four timbered with spacers (see diagrams III-V).

5. Pick up the first upright timbered and swing in front of three, behind one, and out (see diagram VI). Timber down the next standing upright to be a partner with the swinger (see diagram VII). See story on page 33.

II. *The spacers are shaded in the diagram below. Standing uprights are indicated by black circles.*

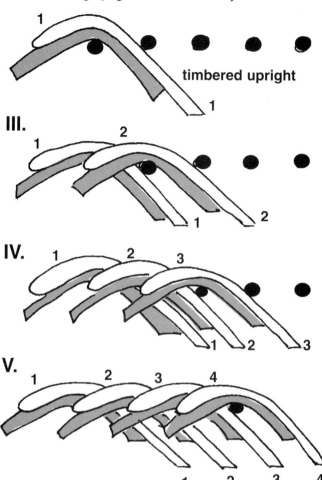

timbered upright

I. **Beginning space for last swinger and timber.**

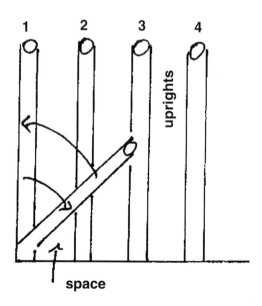

space

VI. Swing in front three, behind one, and out.
The spacers are shaded in the diagram below. The active swinger is black. Timber is striped.

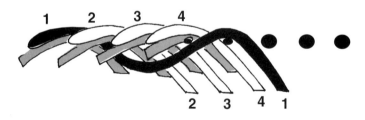

VII. Timber behind one, join swinger.

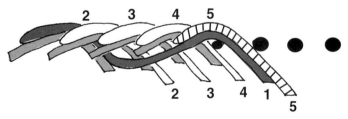

FOUR-ROD TURNDOWN 1-3 USING SPACERS *continued*

FOUR-ROD TURNDOWN 1-3 USING SPACERS *continued*

6. Continue to swing in front of three and out (see diagram VIII), timbering down the uprights as you go (see diagram IX).

VIII. **Continue to swing.**

The spacers are shaded in the diagram below. The active swinger is black. Timber is striped.

swinging uprights

IX.

timbered upright ↓

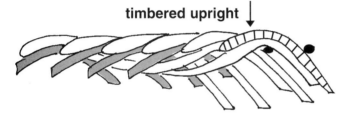

7. When you have eight uprights timbered, you will have four with spacers and four with partners (doubles). From this point on, when you swing, you pick up the inside swinger of the pair. (The one to the right of the pair.) The proper swinger is the one that has only timbered but not swung yet.

8. Continue to swing and timber, keeping the swinger on the outside of the pair. The last upright standing will timber behind one, and go with the swinger behind and under the first timbered upright where you made space at the very beginning (see diagram X).

9. When all uprights are timbered, you are ready to replace the spacers with the corresponding swinger to complete the border pattern (see diagram XI).

10. Check your border before trimming. Save the willow cut off the border for the removable bottom rim if weaving a rim.

X. **Last swinger and timber.**

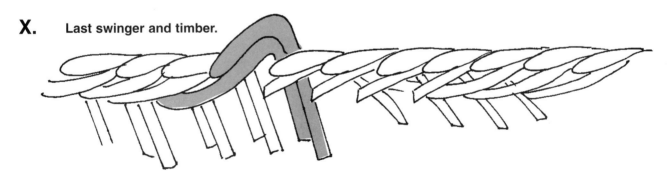

XI. **Replace spacers with proper swinger.**

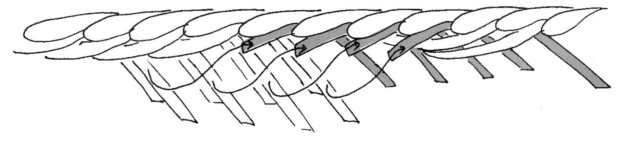

FIVE-ROD TURNDOWN 2-3 USING SPACERS

1. Each upright will timber behind two, swing in front of three, behind two and out. After an upright timbers, it becomes a swinger.

2. Pre-bend the first two uprights because you will need space near the end of your border to thread willows through (see diagram I below).

3. Timber the first upright behind two and out. Place a spacer, the same thickness as the upright, to the front of the timbered upright (see diagram II).

4. Do the same with four more consecutive uprights for a total of five timbered with spacers (see diagrams III-VI).

5. Pick up the first upright timbered and swing in front of three, behind two and out (see diagram VII). Timber down the next standing upright to be a partner with the swinger (see diagram VIII).

6. Continue to swing in front of three and out, timbering down the uprights as you go.

II. *The spacers are shaded in the diagram below.*

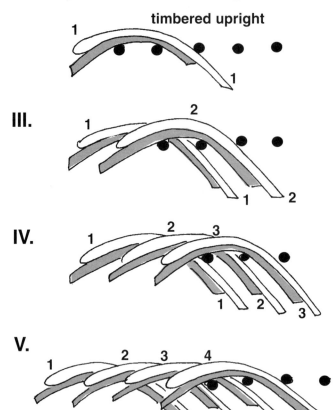

III.

IV.

V.

VI.

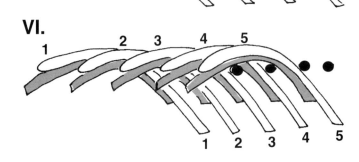

I.

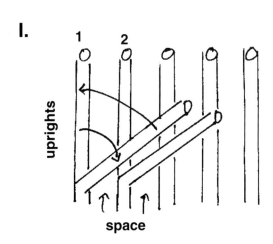

VII. *The active swinger is black. Timber is striped.*

VIII.

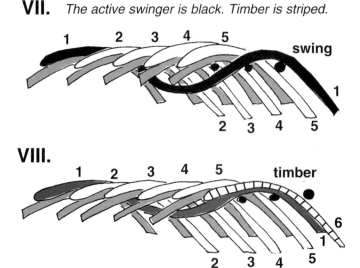

FIVE-ROD TURNDOWN 2-3 USING SPACERS *continued*

swing

7. When you have ten uprights timbered, you will have five with spacers and five with partners (doubles). From this point on, when you swing you pick up the inside swinger of the pair (the one to the right of the pair). The proper swinger is the one which only timbered but not swung yet.

8. Continue to swing and timber keeping the swinger on the outside of the pair. The last uprights will timber behind two and go with the swinger behind and under the first and second timbered uprights where you made space at the very beginning (see diagrams IX-XI).

9. When all uprights are timbered, you are ready to replace the spacers with the corresponding swinger to complete the border pattern (see diagram XII).

10. Check your border before trimming. Save the willow cut off the border for the removable bottom rim if weaving a rim (see diagram XIII).

IX. *The spacers are shaded light gray. Timbers are shaded black. The swingers are darker gray.*

X.

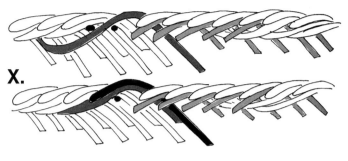

XI. last swinger and timber

XII. replacing the spacers

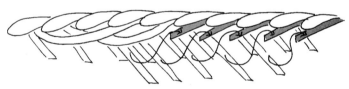

XIII. check border

REMOVABLE BOTTOM RIM

All willow baskets, made in the tradition of the Amana Colonies, have a removable bottom rim. This is an added weaving and turndown that keeps the bottom of the basket off the floor or ground. The rim takes the wear and tear of daily use, and when the rim breaks or wears down you can just remove the old rim and replace it with a new rim.

1. **Inserting bottom rim uprights:**
   Turn your basket upside-down so that you can work on the bottom rim. Slype the uprights you just cut off the top of your basket. Insert one upright along-side each basket side upright, making sure the inserted rim upright is into the basket about 1 to 1 1/2 inches. Be sure that the rim upright is alongside the side upright and not poking out the inside or outside of the basket (see diagram I).

2. **Weaving:** When all rim uprights have been inserted, weave one or two rows of four-rod wale (see page 26) inserting butt, tip, butt, tip (see diagram II). Make sure the weavers are wedged between the base weaving and rim upright (see diagram III). When you weave, push and pull the weaving nice and tight in the proper place (between base weaving and rim uprights). If you do not wedge the weaving in the proper place you may have a gap between the removable bottom rim and the bottom of the basket.

3. **Removable bottom rim border:**
   Timber and swing the rim uprights. A usual removable bottom rim border is timber behind two, swing in front of two, behind two and out. Pound down the bottom rim for that final tightening and leveling (see diagram IV).

I. View: top of basket
Base spokes indicated by black circles.

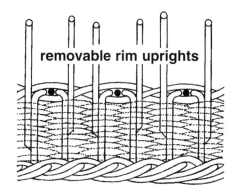

removable rim uprights

II. **Color key for diagrams II-III:** ▨▨▨▨■
Base spokes—15% gray; Side uprights—30% gray Weavers—60% gray; Rim uprights—black

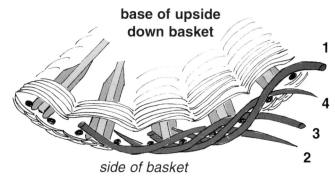

base of upside down basket

1

4

3

2

side of basket

III. *View: looking down on basket bottom*

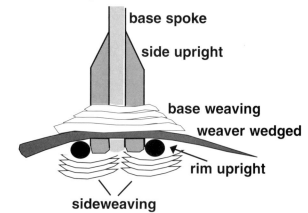

base spoke

side upright

base weaving

weaver wedged

rim upright

sideweaving

IV. **Bottom rim border.**

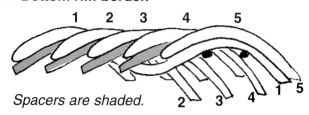

1 2 3 4 5

Spacers are shaded. 2 3 4 1 5

HANDLES

WOODEN PEGGED HANDLE

Wooden handles can be purchased from most basket supply companies. Hoops can be soaked and unglued for a very curved handle.

Wooden handles are usually placed between two uprights (see diagram I), before or after a few rows are woven on the side of the basket. The handle may have to be tapered to fit between the two uprights. After the handle is in place (can be held in place with temporary tape or string), the two uprights and the handle are considered as one upright when you weave the sides.

Before turning down for the top border, the upright to the left of the handle is cut off. The handle and the upright on the right are considered one with the upright timbering and the other border weavers going in front of or behind the handle.

Handle has one or two holes drilled for pegging or wiring into the completed basket side (see diagram II).

Skinny wooden handles can be placed alongside an upright on the completed basket and pegged or wired into place. Ends of the skinny wooden handle must be tapered to go into the small area of the basket with ease and not distort the shape.

FAT HEAVY WILLOW HANDLE

A fat, heavy willow, or other round natural material, if pliable, can be shaped to be used as a handle. The handle bow is placed down the side of an upright on a completed basket. Holes are drilled for pegs or wires (see diagram III).

I. Handle between two uprights.

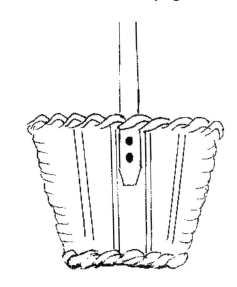

II. Peg placement.

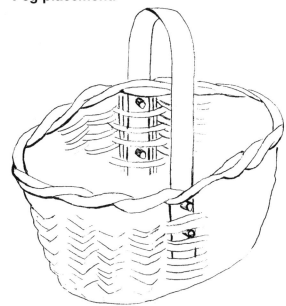

III. Fat willow handle pegged in.

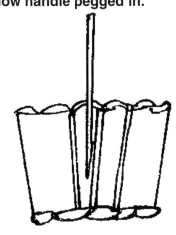

WOODEN HANDLE ATTACHED TO WOODEN BASE

"D" handles (see diagram to the right), if the proper size can be attached to the bottom of a wooden base before any weaving is done. "D" handles with a glued, spliced bottom, if slightly too small, can be soaked to unglue or stretched to attach to the wooden bottom. Be sure to leave space the thickness of weavers between the handle and wood base.

IV. "D" handles

View: Bottom of base

View: Cross-section of basket with a "D" handle.

handles nailed onto base

wooden base

space

handles nailed onto base

ENTWINED

Simple handle using willows that are very flexible. Not a strong handle. Used only on light work baskets. You will be entwining two willows for the handle bow and using those same willows for the handle wrappers. More willow can be added and wrapped around the handle's bow for a fuller handle. The handle will not be as "tidy-neat" as wrapped or twisted handles.

Find opposite timbered uprights so that your handle is balanced and looks even. Pre-open the space with a fat awl or bodkin.

Select two heavy good willows without defects, the same size and length. Slype the butt ends and place one in each handle space (see diagram V-a).

Tie a big single knot with the two handle willows on the very top middle, pulling until the willows are the height of the handle of your basket (see diagram V-b).

Gently circle one willow one or two times around the other willow, working down towards the point of beginning. Thread through the sides from outside to inside the basket. Stay to the left of the handle/upright (see diagram V-c). Stop and do other side the same number of loops (see diagram V-d).

Pick up the handle/wrapper from the inside of the basket, move forward to the front of the handle. Using the willow from the

V. Base spokes are shaded.

a.

b.

c.

d.

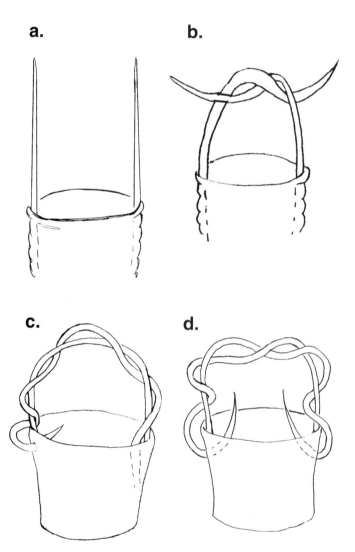

40

HANDLES *continued*

ENTWINED HANDLE *continued*

handle bow, circle back over the handle to the opposite side. Repeat with other handle/wrapper (see diagram V-e).

If you would like your handle filled more, you can insert another handle wrapper on each side and take the wrapper over to the other side, following the flow of the previous willows as much as possible. Insert into the basket from outside to inside, alongside the first wrapper. Repeat on other side of handle.

When you have the handle as full as you want, the tip ends of the wrappers can be finished off simply by threading them into the side weaving. OR thread them around the basket handle before hiding them into the side weaving.

e.

WRAPPED

Simple wrapped handle is easier than a twisted wrapped handle. Only can be used when one high handle is put on a basket. Probably needs over 6 inches between top of basket and top of handle. If your curve is too small in circumference, the simple wrapped handle will not work and you will need a twisted wrapped handle or another material to wrap the small handle.

Select one heavy willow for handle bow or two medium willows for one handle bow.

Choose your placement carefully. Your handle bow will be placed alongside two

opposite timbered uprights. Make space with a fat awl or bodkin.

Gently pre-bend handle bow over knees, with the curve if your basket is curvy, against the curve for very straight handle bow sides.

Insert slyped butt end partway, sliding alongside the uprights. Measure over to opposite side, slype end and insert partway. Finish placing handle bow into basket, pushing both sides at once, or one side a little then the other side a little, until the handle bow is in place.

Select eight long, evenly matched, wrapping willows. They should be as close to perfect as possible. Slype butt ends. Insert two handle wrappers towards the left side of one end of the handle bow (see diagram I). Warm up the willow by running your hand up the two wrappers that are held together. Do not go up and down, since you might kink the willow on the down stroke.

I. Two handle
wrappers inserted.

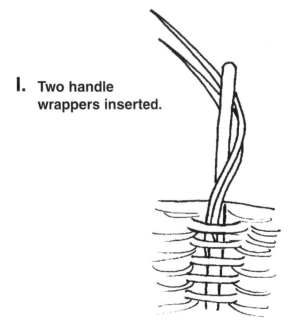

Holding the two wrappers together, start snaking around the handle bow three times with the second turn on the top (sometimes I go around four or five times, depending of the height of the handle bow). Place wrappers in the inside of the basket

HANDLES *continued*

(see diagram II). Do the same on the other side, following the first wrappers.

Insert wrappers on each side through the basket sides, a couple rows down from inside to outside.

Insert one wrapper on each side next to the present wrappers and snake around handle bow, following existing wrappers inside, outside and the basket sides.

Because the curve under the handle bow is a smaller circumference, it will fill faster than the curve on top of the handle bow. If the handle is not full and will accommodate two more wrappers, insert and move over handle bow. If the handle just needs one more wrapper to fill in space, use one but only go to basket top and the finishing tying will hold in place.

There are several ways to tie in the tips of the handle wrappers. Be sure the ends are well-moistened if using peeled willow before tying the tie. Lock ends in place by weaving into existing side weaving or tucking under the existing tie (see diagram III).

II. Two wrappers.

III. Four ways to finish loose handle wrapper ends.

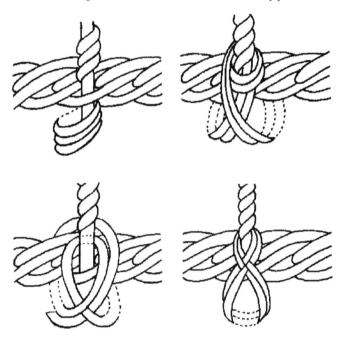

SELF-HANDLE

You need at least one row of waling below, and one row above a "Self Handle."

Weave a complete row of three-rod or four-rod wale. Insert spacers where you want your handle space to be. Use willow or other material.

Weave second row of three-rod or four-rod wale going up and over the spacers.

Border down top.

Clip or remove spacers. You will then have self-handle spaces.

I. Self-handle

Spacers are shaded.

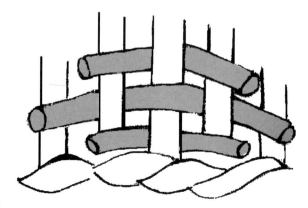

FAKE TWISTED WRAPPED

Cranking willow (technique of twisting willow), to make the twisted, wrapped short handles, is not for the beginner. Cranking is a technique that takes much practice while you waste a lot of willows.

What can a beginner do if they want a twisted short handle? Make a "fake" twisted wrapped handle with round reed. Is using round reed ok? Of course—why not—you will find short reed handles on antique willow baskets. When you are ready to begin learning cranking techniques you will already know how to wrap the twisted willow around the handle.

Handle bow: Using #6 or #7 round reed measure, taper-cut ends and insert into basket. Usually, you have three finger spaces between the basket top border and the inside curve of the handle (see diagram I-a).

Handle wrappers: Insert one long piece of #5 or #6 round reed for wrapper. Wrap around handle bow to the other side. Thread through the basket a couple rows down from basket top to the inside of the basket (see diagram I-b). Bring wrapper up and wrap back to the beginning, through basket side (see diagram I-c). Keep going back and forth until handle is filled (see diagram I-d). The inside circumference of the handle bow will fill faster than the top circumference. You may have hairline spaces between your wrappers. This is OK. It is better to have a neat handle than one that is filled, but bumpy.

I.

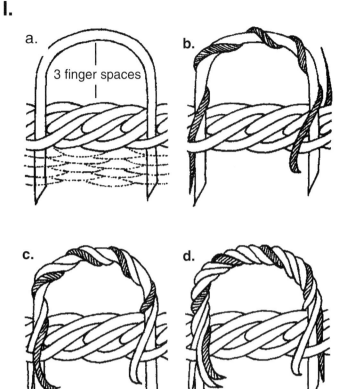

RECIPES

I would like to use "Recipes" instead of "patterns." After you learn willow techniques making "recipe baskets," you are free to weave willow baskets creating your own "recipes," being limited only by the size and amount of your willows. Consider the following "recipes" as a guide to learning the willow techniques as outlined in this book. Refer to the willow techniques as often as you need. Re-read the chapter on "Shaping" before beginning each basket to help you as you weave.

I am still having fun creating baskets, combining wood and willow, and experimenting with willow alone. Do not be afraid to experiment or try new techniques on your own. If you like the results, do it again. If you do not like the results, analyze what you did and maybe change something. Most of all have fun.

When you are ready to do traditional willow baskets, or more difficult baskets, check out *Willow Basketry of the Amana Colonies*, my first book with history and patterns weaving the traditional German willow baskets.

Exposed Base Recipes
Flower Pot
Oval Waste Basket
Oval Wall/Desk Basket

Enclosed Base Recipes
Round Pie/Table Top Basket
Oval Tray
Oval Tote Basket
Five-Gallon Bucket Basket
Rectangular Serving Tray

"Bare Bottom" Recipes
Round Basket
Arm Basket
Heart Basket
Laundry

Woven Base Recipes
Willow I
Willow II
Willow III
Round Willow Basket With Wrapped Handle
Oval Willow Basket with Wooden Handle
Oval Willow Basket with Wrapped Handle

EXPOSED BASE RECIPES

Influenced by a husband, who works with Iowa solid hardwoods, I have always experimented with wood and willow combinations. Exposed bases came from that experimenting. The wood makes the base heavy for baskets that sit on the floor. The uprights tend to stay straight up so exposed bases are not for baskets you want to flare out. Wood thicknesses of 1/2 or 2/3 inch look best.

I try to use willow that goes with the wood color: walnut and steamed willow; cherry or mahogany and buff willow; and poplar, maple or oak with white willow. All the recipes with exposed bases can be made as enclosed base baskets also. If you use the same size base you will end up with a larger basket in width and length. Enjoy experimenting and learning about willow with the "exposed bottoms," or nicknamed "Moon Baskets."

EXPOSED BASE FLOWER POT

Flower pots come in a variety of sizes. Plan your basket around the size you want. This recipe is for 7 inch top diameter, 5 inch diameter bottom pot with drain tray.

SORT AND SOAK:
3 to 4 foot willows to length
    16 for 14 uprights
    16 for 14 French randing
    16 more, may need second set of
        French randing
    21 for three-rod wale
Total: 55 to 70 peeled or unpeeled

BASE:
    Wooden base 6 1/2 inches round with
    14 holes drilled for exposed base.

UPRIGHTS:
    Uprights inserted and bordered bottom
    for exposed base. Use flower pot as
    mold with something heavy inside to
    add weight for stability.

SIDEWEAVING:
    Three-rod wale beginning with tips one
    set, weave to butts, splice butts, weave
    to tips, splice tips, weave to butts, splice
    butts, and weave to tips.

FRENCH RANDING:
    Beginning with 1-1: May use white
    willow or a different color willow.
    Add second set of French randing,
    if you need more height before the
    next weave.

THREE-ROD WALE:
    Beginning with tips, weave to butts,
    splice butts, weave to tips.

BORDER:
    1-2 Crammed or 1-2-1 with spacers.

EXPOSED BASE OVAL WASTE BASKET

Size of wastebasket can vary. I once made one that would hold a brown paper sack from the grocery store. This one is sized to use the plastic bags one gets from the grocery store.

SORT AND SOAK:
4 to 5 foot peeled and unpeeled willows to length
    24 for 22 unpeeled uprights
    24 for 22 unpeeled French randing
    24 for 22 peeled French randing
    24 for 22 second set of peeled French randing
    8 unpeeled four-rod wale
    6 peeled three-rod wale
Total: 56 unpeeled and 54 peeled

BASE:
    9x12 inch round oval (9-inch circle stretched out to 12 inches) 22 holes drilled for exposed base.

UPRIGHTS:
    Inserted and bordered bottom as instructed for exposed base.

SIDEWEAVING:
FRENCH RANDING
    Inserted 2-1: Weave the first, second, and third row 2-1, then switch to French randing weave 1-1.

THREE ROD WALE:
    Two sets of weavers beginning with butts and weaving to tips making one or two rows, depending on length of weavers.

FRENCH RANDING:
    Weavers beginning 2-1 and weaving 1-1.

FOUR-ROD WALE:
    Beginning with butt, tips, butt, tips, weaving one row. Match up ending weavers with beginning weavers.

FRENCH RANDING:
    Beginning with 1-1 and weaving 1-1.

FOUR ROD WALE:
    Beginning with butt, tips, butt, tips, weaving one row.

BORDER: Crammed border 2-3 or 1-3-1 with spacers.

EXPOSED BASE OVAL WALL/DESK BASKET

Size of this basket can be changed after you experience the recipe size.

SORT:

3 to 4 foot willows to length
    22 for 20 unpeeled uprights
    2 heavy peeled willow for entwined handle
    22 for 20 unpeeled French randing
    12 unpeeled for three-rod wale
    6 peeled for accent three-rod wale
Total: 60 to 64 peeled or unpeeled

BASE:

    5x11-inch round oval with 20 holes drilled as instructed for exposed base. Total of 20 holes (see diagram II on page 48).

UPRIGHTS:

    Inserted and bordered as for exposed base using unpeeled willows EXCEPT in hole marked with "X." Insert the heavy white uprights in the two holes marked "X" (see diagram II on page 48). The white uprights in those two holes will designate the back of this wall basket and later become the entwined handle.

SIDEWEAVING:

    Before beginning sideweaving, insert a by-stake on the left side of the two white entwined handle uprights. Consider the white and by-stake as one when weaving. The by-stake will be part of the border.

    FRENCH RANDING:

        Insert 2-1, weave the first and second rows 2-1, then switch to 1-1 weaving.

    THREE-ROD WALE:

        Please read entire directions refering to wooden base diagram before beginning so that you will know

what will happen: Begin first set of three-rod wale on upright A1. Weave one complete row ending where you began. Begin second set of three-rod wale on upright A2, BUT weave from right to left one row—opposite direction or reverse (see diagram I).

I.   **Reverse three-rod wale**
Uprights are indicated by black circles.

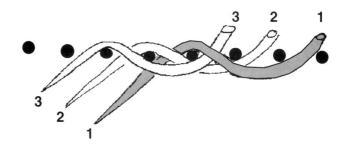

EXPOSED BASE OVAL WALL/DESK BASKET
continued

EXPOSED BASE OVAL WALL/DESK BASKET *continued*

This is reversing the flow of the three-rod wale weavers and creates an arrow pattern (see basket photo on page 47).

II.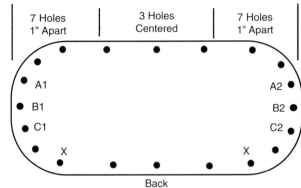

WHITE THREE-ROD WALE:
Begin white three-rod wale on the upright B1 and weave one row. If the white willows are long enough, weave past your beginning, creating a thin row of weaving with tips to back side. Insert second set of white three-rod wale on B2 upright and weave backwards for one row plus the extra length in back. YOU ARE CREATING A HIGHER BACK. This is correct.

UNPEELED THREE-ROD WALE:
Begin on C1 upright and weave for one row. Begin reverse or backward three-rod wale on C2 end and weave one row.

BORDER:
2-3-2 with spacers or crammed. DO NOT USE THE WHITE UPRIGHT. Ignore the white upright and weave border around the white upright.

HANDLE:
Using the white uprights, weave an ENTWINED handle. Add another white willow to entwine if needed or if you want a heavier handle.

ENCLOSED BASE RECIPES

I began enclosed bases when I first started weaving with reed because I did not like the base showing. Transferring knowledge of enclosed bases to willow was easy. With the traditional German removable bottom rim, enclosed bottom baskets become a very

usable, easy to make basket. Willow weaving students who are in a class with very limited time, learn several willow techniques while they are learning to handle willow. Let your imagination wander. After you weave enclosed recipes, create your own.

ROUND PIE TABLE-TOP BASKET

This basket is very useful.
The size can be varied with some planning.

SORT AND SOAK:
3 to 4 foot peeled and unpeeled willows to length
    22 for 20 unpeeled uprights
    22 for 20 peeled French randing
    10 unpeeled willows for three-rod and
        four-rod wale
    12 peeled willows for three-rod wale
Total: 32 unpeeled; 34 peeled

BASE:
    1/4-inch plywood 10 inches round with
    22 holes, approximately 1 1/4 inches
    apart except between holes number 10
    and 11, and holes number 22 and 1,
    which should have spacing of 1 7/8
    inches to accommodate the handle.

HANDLE:
    10 inches tall, square, rounded handle
    (rounded handle with square corners)
    that is glued on bottom splice as
    instructed for attached wooden handle.

UPRIGHTS:
    Uprights inserted for enclosed base.

SIDEWEAVING:
    THREE-ROD WALE:
        Unpeeled willow two beginnings
        with butts weaving to tips.

    FRENCH RANDING:
        Peeled willow insert 2-1 and
        weave 1-1.

THREE-ROD WALE:
    Peeled willow two beginning with
    tips, weave to butts, splice butts and
    weave to tips. Should have two rows.

BORDER:
    1-3-1 with spacers.

REMOVABLE BOTTOM RIM: "EXPOSED"
    The exposed removable bottom rim
    will show on the outside of the basket,
    resting on the crack of French randing.
    Insert removable rim uprights from
    bottom up through rod wale weaving
    and French randing insert, on top of
    French randing crack, into top rod
    waling (see basket photo above). Weave
    one row of weaving and turn down rim.

HANDLE:
    Was inserted at the very beginning.

OVAL TRAY

SORT AND SOAK:

3 foot willows to length

    28 for 26 heavy uprights unpeeled

    28 for 26 French randing peeled

    12 unpeeled willows for three-rod wale

    4 to 8 for removable bottom rim weavers

Total: 40 unpeeled; 36 peeled

BASE:

    9x11-inch plywood base with 26 holes.

UPRIGHTS:

    Inserted 26 uprights as instructions for enclosed base.

SIDEWEAVING:

PEELED FRENCH RANDING:

    Insert 2-1. Make sure the butt is wedged between the base and uprights. Weave first row 2-1, then weave 1-1.

THREE-ROD WALE:

    Beginning with tips weave to butts. After one complete row, insert spacers for "SELF-HANDLE." Continue with three-rod wale. Splice butt, weave to tips. Splice tips or butts, depends on the height. You want only three complete rows of three-rod wale ending with tips.

BORDER:

    1-2 crammed.

REMOVABLE BOTTOM RIM:

    One row of weaving. Border 1-2 crammed.

OVAL TOTE BASKET

SORT AND SOAK:

4 to 5 foot peeled and unpeeled willows to length

    22 for 20 unpeeled or peeled uprights.
        (Your choice.)

    22 for 20 for French randing
        (13 peeled and 9 unpeeled)

    16 to 22 unpeeled three-rod wale
        and four-rod wale

    18 to 24 peeled three-rod wale

    Approximately 80 inches of shaker
        tape for handles

Total: 90 peeled or unpeeled

BASE:

    6x10 inches with 20 holes drilled as
    instructed for enclosed base.

UPRIGHTS:

    Inserted for enclosed base. Gathered and
    tied.

HANDLE:

    Clothespin shaker tape to willows where
    you would like your handles. Begin on
    bottom base, up side upright, loop,
    down sides upright but on same side as
    up, across bottom to other side. Up
    upright, loop, down upright, back to
    beginning. Tape will be tacked to
    bottom board.

SIDEWEAVING:

THREE-ROD WALE:

    Unpeeled willows two beginnings
    with tips. Weave to butts. Splice
    butts weave to tips. Splice tips,
    weave to butts, splice butts, to tips.
    ADJUST HANDLE MAKING
    LOOPS EVEN.

FRENCH RANDING:

    Insert 1-1 beginning with 3 peeled,
    then 2 unpeeled, 3 peeled, 2 unpeeled,
    etc,. Weave 1-1.

THREE-ROD WALE:

    Peeled willow two beginnings. Tip to
    butt. Butt to tip. Tip to butt. Butt to tip.

BORDER:

    1-3-1 with spacers. Fold the shaker tape
    on the inside or outside of the basket
    and border around.

REMOVABLE BOTTOM RIM:

    Use peeled or unpeeled for weavers.

FIVE-GALLON BUCKET BASKET

This basket which holds a five-gallon bucket is great for paper trash, kindling wood, etc. The basket is large enough to be a small laundry hamper if you keep the inside smooth.

SORT AND SOAK:
4 to 6 foot willows to length
   30 for 28 heavy, unpeeled uprights
   30 for 28 French randing
      (15 unpeeled, 15 peeled)
   30 for 28 second set of French
      randing peeled willow
   8 peeled willow for four-rod wale
   32 unpeeled
   32 peeled
   One long piece of #6 round reed for handle
   One heavy willow for handle bow
Total: 78 unpeeled; 85 peeled

BASE:
   Using bucket size of 11 1/2 inches top, 13 inches high, trace bottom 11 inches. Center of your holes should be 1/2 inch out from bottom tracing plus another 1/2 inch of wood. Plywood board will be a 12 to 12 1/4 inch circle with 28 holes.

UPRIGHTS:
   Inserted as for enclosed base.

INSERT FIVE GALLON BUCKET WITH WEIGHT TO USE AS FORM:
   Bucket probably will stay put on the inside of your bordered uprights.

SIDEWEAVING:
FOUR-ROD WALE 2-2:
   Two sets beginning with tips. Weave to butts, splice butts back to tips. Again, tips to butts, butts to tips.

FOUR-ROD WALE 3-1:
   One row of peeled four-rod wale beginning butt, tip, butt, tip. Matching ending with beginning.

FRENCH RANDING:
   Alternating peeled and unpeeled. Insert 1-1 and weave 1-1.

FOUR ROD WALE 3-1:
   One row of peeled four-rod wale beginning butt, tip, butt, tip, matching ending with beginning.

FRENCH RANDING:
   Using peeled willows inserting 2-1 and weaving 1-1.

THREE-ROD WALE:
   Two sets beginning with tips weave to butts, splice butts and back to tips. Add another group of three-rod wale if you need to add more height to basket.

BORDER:
   2-3-2 with spacers.

REMOVABLE BOTTOM RIM:
   One row peeled four-rod wale beginning butt, tip, butt, tip. Matching ending with beginnings. Border rim with 2-2-2 spacers.

HANDLE:
   One fake twisted handle using willow spoke and #6 round reed, dyed to match willow for wrapped handle. Suggest 3 to 4 upright spaces between handle spoke.

RECTANGULAR SERVING TRAY

SORT AND SOAK:
5 to 6 foot peeled and unpeeled willows
    46 for 44 unpeeled uprights
    46 for 44 peeled French randing
    20 unpeeled three-rod and four-rod
Total: 46 peeled; 66 unpeeled

BASE:
    11x14-inch plywood rectangle with clipped corners. Three corner holes 3/4 inch apart center to center. Nine additional holes spaced on long side. Seven additional holes on short side.

UPRIGHTS:
    Unpeeled, inserted as instructed for enclosed base.

SIDEWEAVING:
FRENCH RANDING:
    Using peeled willows, be sure the beginnings are between wood board and upright. Insert 2-1. Weave first row 2-1 then, weave 1-1.

THREE-ROD WALE:
    Two beginnings with tips in the middle of long side. Both sets complete one row.

SELF-HANDLE:
    Insert spacers for handle NOW.

THREE-ROD WALE:
    Continue weaving splicing butts. Weave up over spacers for self-handle.

BORDER:
    1-3-1 with spacers.

REMOVABLE BOTTOM RIM:
    Unpeeled weavers.

 **NOTES**

"BARE BOTTOM" RECIPES

One year at an *Association of the Michigan Basketmaker Convention*, Rachel Nash Law gave a slide show of old museum baskets. She made the comment that whenever she thinks she has come up with a new idea or technique in basketry, she finds an old antique basket with the same idea or technique she thought was original. I believe this is very true. Nothing is ever new in basketry. Just revived, renamed, or renewed.

Wooden bottom willow baskets are one example. I have been experimenting and perfecting "Bare Bottom" willow baskets for several years. At the *1995 Willow Weekend*, a student brought an antique willow basket from Wyoming to show me. It had a wooden base with holes and willow uprights, just like my "Bare Bottom" baskets. As this book was in progress, I found a round, cornered, rectangular, wooden bottom, antique, willow laundry basket at a local shop. I have included my version of both wooden bottom baskets in this book. Revived as "Bare Bottom" baskets.

ROUND BASKET

SORT AND SOAK:
4 foot peeled willows to length
    18 for 16 uprights
    18 for 16 French randing
    20 for base border/three-rod wale
Total: without handle—56 to 60 willows;
    peeled or unpeeled

    For two handles: 2 willow handle bows
        and two lengths of #5 round reed
    For one handle: 1 willow handle bow
        and 8-10 perfect long willows

BASE:
    8 inch circle solid wood base with 16 holes drilled for "Bare Bottom" instructions. Pricked, gathered and tied up.

SIDEWEAVING:
    Two sets of four-rod wale BASE BORDER beginning with four butts. Continue with three-rod wale.

THREE ROD WALE:
    Continue weaving the two sets of three-rod wale, splicing butts each time, until you have 1 1/2 to 2 inches of weaving.

FRENCH RANDING:
    Insert 1-1, weave 1-1.

BORDER:
    1-3-1 with spacers or one of the crammed borders.

HANDLE:
    Can be added. Two short using reed or one long using willow.

ARM BASKET

SORT AND SOAK:
5 to 6 foot willows to length
    22 for 20 peeled upright
    22 for 20 peeled French randing
    30 unpeeled willows for four-rod
        and three-rod
    One fat handle bow
    8 perfect peeled willows for handle wraps
Total: 52 peeled, 31 unpeeled

BASE:
    9x11 round oval solid wood base with 20 holes drilled for "Bare Bottom." Center hole on long side for handle placement.

UPRIGHTS:
    Insert 20 peeled uprights as "Bare Bottom" instructions. Gather and tie up.

SIDEWEAVING:
    Two sets of four-rod wale BASE BORDER beginning with four butts, using unpeeled willow. Continue with three-rod wale.

THREE-ROD WALE:
    Continue weaving the two sets of three-rod wale, splicing butts each time until you have 3 1/2 to 4 inches of weaving.

FRENCH RANDING:
    Peeled willow insert 2-1, weave 1-1.

FOUR-ROD WALE:
    Beginning with butt, tip, butt, tip; matching ending with beginning.

BORDER:
    1-3-1 with spacers.

HANDLE:
    Wrapped handle.

 **NOTES**

HEART BASKET

From the bottom of my heart.

SORT AND SOAK:
3 foot willows to length
    (2 foot can also be used)
    24 for 22 peeled uprights
    24 for 22 French randing
      unpeeled
    8 for base border/three-rod
      unpeeled
Total: 24 peeled, 32 unpeeled

BASE:
    Seven-inch wide heart with 22 holes.
    Hint: Flatten the point of the heart
    slightly for easy drilling. Keep holes
    small enough to hold uprights tightly.

UPRIGHTS:
    Insert as "Bare Bottom" instructions.
    Do not forget to push upright in hole
    before each prick up (bending up).

SIDEWEAVING:
    BASE BORDER four-rod wale, two
    beginnings with tips. One beginning

at bottom of heart and one at top indent
of heart. Continue with three-rod wale
until you have two complete rows.

FRENCH RANDING:
    Insert 1-1 and weave 1-1. Stop
    French randing after seven rows.

BORDER:
Heart on left in above photo:
    2-3-2 with spacers.
Heart on right in above photo:
    Behind one then cut resting on
    upright.

 **NOTES**

LAUNDRY

SORT AND SOAK:
5 to 6 foot willows to length
    34 for 32 peeled uprights
       (can be unpeeled also)
    34 for 32 French randing, peeled
    34 for 32 second set of French
       randing, peeled
    20 peeled for four-rod wale
    8 white peeled for four-rod wale
    2 heavy handle bows
    2 #6 round reed for wrapped handle
Total: 122 peeled, 8 contrasting peeled

BASE:
    9 1/2 x 18-inch solid wood board
    with 1 1/2 inch radius corners.
    Holes: One in each corner and one on
    each side of corner hole, 1 inch away.
    Seven additional holes on long side and
    three additional holes on short side.
    Total of holes: 32.

UPRIGHTS:
    Insert 32 uprights as "Bare Bottom"
    instructions. Gather and tie up with
    three ties: Middle uprights, and two
    end uprights.

SIDEWEAVING:
    FOUR-ROD WALE:
        Two beginnings with butt, tip, butt,
        tip. Need two or three rows to be
        above wooden base.

    FRENCH RANDING:
        Because this is a laundry basket and
        you want the inside to be as smooth
        as possible, French randing butts will
        need to be on the outside of the

basket. Insert all 32 French randings;
butt out, behind one, and out.
(see diagram I-II). Weave first row
2-1, then 1-1. Butts are inserted on
the outside so that the inside of the
basket is smooth.

SECOND SET OF FRENCH RANDING:
    Again, insert all 32 French randing
    weavers so their butts are on the
    outside. First row weave 1-1 and
    continue weaving 1-1.

THREE-ROD WALE:
    Using contrasting white willow, two
    beginnings with tips to butt, splice
    butts, back to tips.

BORDER:
1-3-1 with spacers.

HANDLES:
Two short, fake handles on the long side.
You will be able to walk easily through
the doorway with your laundry basket
if the handles are on the long side.

I. **French randing inserted outside of side uprights.**

View: side view

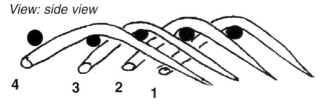

II.

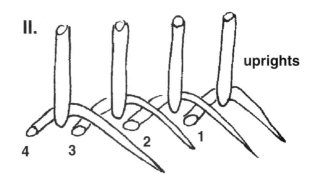

uprights

WOVEN BASE RECIPES

Hopefully you have woven with willow before you embark on willow bases. They are not hard, but when you are first weaving with willow they can be frustrating. By making willow baskets using wooden bases you learned a lot about willow and are now ready to think about woven bases.

The recipes are to help you expand your knowledge. Once you feel comfortable with woven bases, do not be afraid to create your own recipes. Remember, the only limit you will have is the amount and size of your willow.

WILLOW I

Kathy Kellenberger and Joanna Schanz team teach Amana Colony Willow Basketry *to groups of 12 students. Joanna says, "In the past, we have noticed that it was very stressful for students to learn all the techniques in one basket. Just when students would begin to understand one technique, we would stop them and introduce another technique. Because of the time and stress on students, we developed* Willow I *and* Willow II.

Willow I *uses three-rod wale for the sideweaving which is called* Triple Weave *in round reed work. Once students start on three-rod wale, they can weave until it is time to turndown the top border or they run out of weaving willow.* Willow II *teaches French randing."*

SORT AND SOAK:
117 to 120 unpeeled 4 foot willows to length.
  Cut 6 fat base spokes 9 inches long. Place willows left from base spokes in correct sorted pile.
  Choose one very heavy willow for handle spoke. Mark and save.
  8 to 10 nice, long, evenly matched, as close to perfect; mark and save for handle wrappers.
  26 for the 24 heavy long uprights (extra for "just in case").
  The rest will be base weavers and sideweavers.

BASE:
  3/3 base spokes. Start with shortest weavers because you are working in a small circumference. Gradually work your way to longer willow weavers as your circumference gets larger. Weave to 7-inch base.

UPRIGHTS:
Two per base spoke.

BASE BORDER:
  (If you want to weave removable bottom rim, go directly to sideweaving. Do not weave base border.) Begin with two sets of butts; four-rod wale changing to three-rod wale.

SIDEWEAVING:
  THREE-ROD WALE
    Splice butts and always splice butts. Make sure your two sets of weavers are balanced; splicing and ending on opposite sides of the basket. Weave to desired height, but must have at least 12 inches of uprights for top border.

BORDER:
  Crammed or with spacers (your choice).

REMOVABLE BOTTOM RIM:
  If you did not weave Base Border.

HANDLES:
  One wrapped or entwined.

WILLOW II

SORT AND SOAK:

86 to 100 unpeeled willows to length.
 Cut 8 fat base spokes 11 inches.
  Place willows left from base cuttings
  back into sorted piles.
 34 for 32 heavy, long uprights
  (extra for "just in case").
 34 for 32 French randing weavers,
  need to be evenly matched in
  thickness and length.
  Rest are base weavers and
  removable rim weavers.

BASE:
 4/4 base spokes. Weave to 9 inches.

UPRIGHTS:
 Two per base spoke.

SIDEWEAVING:
 FRENCH RANDING:
  One French randing weaver per
  upright. Weave French randing,
  insert 2-1 and weave 1-1 to tips.

THREE-ROD WALE:
 Begin with three tips. Weave to butts.
 Splice butts and weave back to tips.
 You should have two rows.

BORDER:
 Crammed or with spacers (your choice).

REMOVABLE BOTTOM RIM:
 One row weaving-border same as top.

NOTES

WILLOW III
Oval version of three-rod wale

SORT AND SOAK:
112 to 120 unpeeled willows (14 peeled) to length.
   Cut 5 fat base width spokes 8 inches. 3 base length
      spokes 11 inches and two 4 inch spacers.
   Choose one very fat, heavy willow for
      handle spoke
   8 to 10 nice, long, evenly matched,
      as close to perfect for handle wrappers.
   24 for 22 heavy, long uprights
      Approximately 39 three-rod weavers
   14 weavers of contrasting color for accent
      weavers
   16 weavers for base

BASE:
   Insert length (long) base spokes inside
   width (short) base spokes with spacers.
   Weave to 6x9 inch size.

UPRIGHTS:
   One upright for three middle spokes
   on long side. Then 2-1-2-1-2 on curve.

SIDEWEAVING:
   THREE-ROD WALE:
      Begin two sets with tips. Weave to
      butts. Splice butts and weave to tips.
      Continue weaving three-rod wale;
      splicing butts to butts and tips to
      tips. After 8 rows, switch to contrast-
      ing willow, beginning one set with
      butts. Weave halfway and splice
      new set of butts, and weave to begin-
      ning, matching ends with beginnings.

REVERSE THREE-ROD WALE:
   (See diagram I on page 47.)
   Begin butts of three-rod wale but
   weaving in the opposite direction
   halfway. Splice new set of butts, still
   weaving opposite direction, weaving
   to beginning, where you match up
   ends with beginnings.

THREE-ROD WALE:
   Go back to regular three-rod wale
   using original willow for two to
   three rows.

BORDER:
   Your choice—crammed or with spacers.

REMOVABLE BOTTOM RIM:
   Peeled weavers, border same as top
   border.

HANDLE:
   Wrapped or entwined.

ROUND WILLOW BASKET WITH WRAPPED HANDLE

SORT AND SOAK:

120 to 130 willows to length.

Cut 6 fat base spokes, 11 inches.

Place willows left from base cuttings back into sorted piles.

If one handle: choose one very fat, heavy willow for handle spoke and 8 to 10 nice, long, evenly matched, and as close to perfect. Mark and save for handle wrappers.

If 2 small fake handles: choose two heavy willows for handle spoke and 2 long, #5 round reeds.

26 for 24 heavy, long uprights (extra selected)

26 for 24 French randing weavers (13 peeled and 13 unpeeled) need to be evenly matched in thickness and length.

50 to 60 for base weavers, four-rod wale, three-rod wale, and removable bottom rim weavers.

BASE:

3/3 base spokes. Weave to 9 inches. Approximately 20 weavers.

UPRIGHTS:

Two for each base spoke.

SIDEWEAVING:

FOUR-ROD WALE:

Begin two sets with tips. Weave to butts, splice butts, and weave to tips.

FRENCH RANDING:

Insert 1-1 alternating; peeled and unpeeled. Weave 1-1.

THREE-ROD WALE:

Using one set of weavers, beginning with tips. Weave to butts, splice butts and weave to tips.

BORDER:

2-2-2 border with spacers (see diagram IV on page 38).

REMOVABLE BOTTOM RIM:

Unpeeled weavers, same border as top border.

HANDLE: One wrapped or two of fake-twisted wrapped.

OVAL WILLOW BASKET WITH WOODEN HANDLE

SORT AND SOAK:
70 to 100 (8 peeled) willows to length.
  Cut 5 fat base spokes; 7 inches long for
    width, and 3 fat base spokes, 11 inches
    long for length.
  Cut two spacers four inches long.
    26 for 24 heavy, long uprights.
    24 for 22 French randing weavers,
    need to be evenly matched in
    thickness and length.
  40 to 50 for base weavers, three-rod
    wale, French randing, and removable
    bottom rim weavers.

BASE:
  Insert length (long) base spokes inside
  width (short) base spokes with spacer.
  Weave to 5x9 inch size. Approximately
  12 weavers.

UPRIGHTS:
  Uprights inserted so middle base spoke
  has two for handle placement.

SIDEWEAVING:
  THREE-ROD WALE:
    Begin two sets with tips. Weave to
    butts, splice butts, and weave to tips.
    Insert WOODEN HANDLE between
    two uprights. From this position,
    consider the handle and the uprights
    on each side as one upright
    when weaving and turn down.

FRENCH RANDING:
  Insert 2/1 and weave 1/1.

BORDER:
  2-3 crammed border. Cut the uprights on
  the left side of the handle off, and save
  for removable bottom rim, along with
  other cut off border willows.

REMOVABLE BOTTOM RIM:
  Peeled weavers, border same as top
  border.

PEG HANDLE:
  Peg handle in place.

OVAL WILLOW BASKET WITH WRAPPED HANDLE

SORT AND SOAK:

120 to 140 willows (12 peeled) to length.

    Cut 5 fat base width spokes 11 inches,
3 base length spokes 14 inches and two
6 inch spacers.

    Choose one, very fat, heavy willow
for handle spoke.

    8 to 10 nice, long, evenly matched,
as close to perfect for handle
wrappers.

    24 for 22 heavy, long uprights

    24 for 22 French randing weavers, need
to be evenly matched in thickness and
length.

    50 to 60 for base weavers, three-rod wale,
French randing, and removable bottom
rim weavers.

BASE:

    Insert length (long) base spokes inside
width (short) base spokes with spacers.
Weave to 9x12 inch size. Approximately
20 weavers.

UPRIGHTS:

    Uprights inserted so middle width base
spoke has one upright.

SIDEWEAVING:

  FOUR-ROD WALE:

    Begin two sets with tips. Weave to
butts, splice butts, and weave to tips.

  FOUR-ROD WALE USING 2 PEELED
WILLOW:

    Begin with butt, tip, butt, tip.
Matching end with beginning for
one row.

FRENCH RANDING:

    Insert 2/1 and weave 1/1.

THREE-ROD WALE:

    Using two sets of peeled willow
weavers, beginning with butts,
weave to tips.

BORDER:

    2-3 crammed border, or 1-3-1 with
spacers.

REMOVABLE BOTTOM RIM:

    Peeled weavers, border same as top
border.

HANDLE:

    Wrapped, using peeled willows.
Insert fat handle bow and wrap.

Memory of a Willow

Just a timid little sprout, I began in the spring
Embraced by the warmth of the sun.
How I grew.
My roots reached for the moisture below.
I stretched for the sky, day by day,
Time goes by.
Sturdy and strong I have become.
Fall arrives.
I feel the frost.
Too cold for my leaves, they fall to the ground.
Cut and bundled, patiently I wait to be taken on a journey.
Two by two, over and under I go.
I have become a part of this basket you see.
Now that timid little sprout is just a memory to me.

—Laura Kleinmeyer
Willow Basketmaker

NOTES

NOTES

NOTES